THE
HYPNOTISM
HANDBOOK

By CHARLES EDWARD COOKE
and
A. E. VAN VOGT

1965
BORDEN PUBLISHING CO.
Alhambra, California

Second Edition, Tenth Printing

Printed in the United States of America

CONTENTS

vii

THE COOKE HYPNOTIZING SPIRAL

This miniature reproduction of the 12 inch hypnotizing spiral can
be removed, trimmed, and used as a fixation point.

FOREWORD

By a Physician

Until recently, hypnosis has been largely neglected by the medical profession. In my opinion, Mr. Cooke is outstanding in the field of hypnotherapy for psychotherapeutic work. He has achieved this skill through his own initiative coupled with an extensive personal experience, without the advantage of formal psychiatric training.

I routinely employ several of Cooke's techniques which have proved to be consistently effective. Even though I am not qualified as a psychiatrist, but as an interested observer with a medical background, it is my opinion and part of my personal experience that the following observations are valid.

Mr. Cooke emphasizes the importance of the use of specific words as "signals" and "symbolizations" in auto-hypnosis, insomnia, etc. I have found this very effective. Bibliotherapy in patient reeducation to aid them in making mature decisions deserves special attention. The use of "internal" or "body awareness" as a technique for symptom removal or relief, and also as a preliminary to the induction of hypnosis is noteworthy. This method facilitates the management of the extremely self-controlled subject. The author correctly stresses the frequently overlooked point, that the patient in reality actually hypnotizes himself, being aided by the guidance of the instructor. The recognition of this fact by the patient immediately promotes a strong feeling of security and self-confidence. It also decreases his feeling of dependency on the instructor, and thereby automatically becomes an aid in teaching autohypnosis. Cooke exhibits an outstanding ability in presenting a clear word picture to activate the patient's imagination. This fact may, in part, be responsible for his ability to locate and desensitize specific problems and phobias in his subjects.

In my experience I have noted that the vocabulary and phraseology of most physicians, unless they have had psychiatric training, is inadequate to express appropriate suggestions for hypnotherapy. This book presents the precise wording for these suggestions in managing the common office problems. Words can be potent and should be intelligently applied. The average reader will welcome this practical reference book that is readily understandable and not complicated by the use of ultra-scientific jargon, which so commonly prevails in similar books. Certainly Mr. Cooke should be commended for his untiring efforts and foresight in creating this valuable and practical contribution to the progress of hypnosis.

Richard N. Clark, M. D.

Diplomate of the American Board of Obstetrics and Gynecology. Member of The Society for Clinical and Experimental Hypnosis. Instructor of Obstretrics and Gynecology, School of Medicine, University of Southern California.

By a Dentist

The use of hypnosis in dentistry is more widely accepted both by the profession and the public today than ever before. This is probably due to a better understanding of this phenomena and its uses. When it becomes better known by the dentist and he masters its uses, it will be found to be a most valuable addition to his armanentarium.

The techniques as described by Mr. Cooke cover the field very thoroughly. As one becomes more familiar with hypnosis he will adopt variations to suit himself and his patients. In this manual the beginner will find everything needed to get him started. Those using hypnosis in their practice will find it very useful for reference and study.

I would call special attention to the chapters covering the first visit and the awakening.

The description of the first visit with the patient is very complete. It will be necessary to change the wording to suit the dentist rather than the therapist. The important thing that it brings out is the advisability of acquainting the patient with the phenomena, what to expect, and clearing up previous misconceptions. Adequate time spent at this visit will save much valuable time in future visits and insure a high percentage of cooperative patients.

The importance of a good awakening technique can not be over-stressed. I speak as an operator and a subject. Mr. Cooke realizes this and has given a very good word by word description as well as the advantages and reasons.

James M. Hixson, D.M.D., F.A.C.D.

By a Psychologist

Millions of words are in print in all languages, purportedly explaining techniques to be used with various types of hypnotherapy by psychologists, counselors, psychotherapists and physicians who deal with emotionally upset persons. Only a rare few of these books and articles give detailed wordage for actual use when treating a patient by hypnosis.

Charles Cooke has had daily experience for years in the practical phases of helping emotionally disturbed persons to reorient themselves. By actual trial and error, and by trying many patterns of oral phrasing, of beneficial suggestions, he has developed the contents of this book. Psychologists and physicians who have studied the techniques of hypnosis with Cooke have found these phrases of extreme benefit.

Upon reading the manuscript of this book, I was agreeably surprised to find that Cooke had captured in print the essence of the teaching techniques which I have observed while watching him teach the techniques of hypnotherapy. The neophyte hypnotherapist will find here the word pictures which are so essential when using hypnotherapy with an emotionally upset person.

For everyone who contacts daily and intimately the overlapping fields of medicine and psychotherapy, this work, with its emphasis on the specific methods of emotional re-education, is of genuine importance. Modern medicine today avows that every patient must be taught to understand himself if he is to live comfortably and happily in his environment. Hypnotherapy and hypnoanalysis are two additional tools available to all who endeavor to help their fellow humans. This handbook can teach the open-minded clinician more effective and speedier methods of aiding those who come for treatment.

Jean Bordeaux, Ph. D.

Author of "How to Talk More Effectively," "Aphasia Therapeutics," (with Mary Longerich, Ph. D.), "Hypnotism Today" (with Leslie LeCron).

INTRODUCTION

HYPNOSIS BY PRESCRIPTION

In this volume is attempted, possibly for the first time, the venture of putting hypnosis on a prescription basis. It is written primarily to give physicians and psychologists a set of verbal patterns which can be used with precision.

WORD-FOR-WORD INDUCTION TECHNIQUES

Chapter Two is devoted to an exact method of inducing hypnosis and of testing the degree of response in a person of average intelligence. The words of Chapter Two have been used hundreds of times by many therapists. It is possible to create the trance condition merely by *reading* the technique to the subject in a monotonous voice. In lecture halls Cooke has hypnotized with these same words as many as four hundred individuals at once. He has found them equally useful in private practice with those who have come for psychological consultation.

Most published books on hypnosis lack precise methodology. These works devote only a few paragraphs to actual technique. The statement is then made that the time required for induction varies with individuals, and that for difficult subjects the operator may have to urge sleep for an hour or more.

Such sketchily described techniques are of little value to most students.

It is easy to obtain some degree of hypnotic response from almost everyone. According to most authorities one out of every five subjects can be taken "down" to the deep somnabulistic stage the first time. The practitioner then proves to himself and to the subject that the somnambulistic trance has been attained. This he does by a series of tests. For example, on the Davis and Husband susceptibility scoring system, catalepsy of the eyes is given a score of six. It is the earliest "light" trance phenomena, and is challenged firmly with the words: "Your eyelids are sticking tightly, so tightly that you cannot open them. Try to open them, but you cannot. Try hard—but you cannot."

Here the test is comparatively simple. If the hypnosis is effective, the eyelids will stick, and the hypnotist proceeds to the next test.

DEEP TRANCE TESTS

On the same list, the "negative visual hallucination" is given a score of thirty. This can be combined with the auditory, tactile, and other negative hallucinations which have a high score on the Davis and Husband scale. In this test the subject must be induced to ignore with *all* his senses a person or object present throughout the experiment. For the time being the negated object "simply is not there" to the subject.

Such a test requires precise phrasing in the suggestion used.

Similarly, the hypnoanalytic procedures of age regression, automatic writing, dreaming by direction, etc., must be *taught* to the subject. It is important to use the right words.

DEEP TRANCE
NOT NECESSARY FOR THERAPY

In spite of individual variations, the tests are now recognized by all authorities. They constitute a standard by which the hypnotist judges the subject's progress

xvi

from "light" to the "medium" to the "deep" trance states. Fortunately, neither the "medium" nor the "deep" trance is necessary in order to obtain definite benefits. Even in the hypnoidal state, before any tests will "take," the subject is.more responsive to suggestion than normally. Once the hypnosis is induced, results may be obtained by reading aloud to the subject the suggestions given in later chapters.

SUBJECT HYPNOTIZES SELF

In America it has become the practice, psychologically sound, to place the onus for the success of a hypnosis on the subject. This is because, in a theoretical sense, people are not hypnotized. They hypnotize themselves—under the guidance of an operator.

The basic truth of this does not relieve the "guide" of responsibility for the induction. It is the operator's skill that enables a subject to hypnotize himself. A hypnotist is "good" or "bad" depending on the degree of success gained by his subjects,—degree not only as a measure of the percentage who achieve some hypnotic response, but also as a measure of the "depth" achieved and the speed with which it is reached.

HIGH PERCENTAGE OF PEOPLE CAN BE HYPNOTIZED

It is estimated that some 60% of the population can learn under skillful direction to attain the somnambulistic "deep" trance state. According to Dr. J. M Bramwell,[4] who practiced in the first two decades of the century, 80% to 97% are capable of some degree of hypnotic response. More recently LeCron and Bordeaux[21] analyzed available statistics and arrived at the figure of 60% for deep trance and 85% to 90% for light trance or better. The authors add, "While these estimates may err slightly, they are intentionally conservative."

It is well to have these comparisons in mind when assessing one's skill at inducing hypnosis.

MOST PEOPLE NEED PSYCHOTHERAPY

According to Weiss and English,[35] approximately one-third of every physician's patients are in need only of psychotherapy, and another third needs psychotherapy in addition to surgical and medical services. Other authorities largely substantiate these figures.

HYPNOSIS A SHORT CUT

Psychoanalysis as developed by Freud and others is of little value to the average person because treatment is prolonged and expensive. Freud himself recognized this limitation and in 1919 admitted that if psychotherapy were ever to become widely available to the public, a return to hypnosis as a short cut would be necessary.

The modern psychotherapist frequently uses hypnosis in diagnosis. He also uses hypnosis to sharpen and speed up his psychotherapeutic, or psychoanalytic procedure. At times the swiftness with which results are achieved dazzles both the patient and the therapist. At other times much slower results are obtained. When usable, hypnosis makes possible a faster response to therapy.

SUPPORTIVE THERAPY

The traditional form of hypnotherapy was to suggest that the pain was *not* there, that an organ or limb *would* function, that an attitude would change, and so the symptom was charmed away—perhaps. That was the phase of hypnosis which fell into disrepute because the cure was not always permanent. Today "supportive therapy" (formerly called "symptom treatment") is given with the full knowledge that it is not a "cure" but that it does make life more livable.

SOME SPECIFIC CURES

Certain specific uses for heterohypnosis and self-hypnosis lend themselves well to the purposes of every practitioner. Insomnia is endemic in America today. In a high percentage of cases it can be eliminated by hypnosis. Psychiatrists may point out in this connection that insomnia is only one manifestation of anxiety, and that another symptom may replace the inability to sleep. The answer to that is simple. The continual use of hypnosis is *not injurious* but the continual use of barbituates has been condemned by many authoritative sources. We may question whether or not any substitute symptom, with the possible exception of alcoholism and, of course, such drugs as morphine and cocaine, can be as dangerous to the general health as barbiturate addiction.

Alcoholism is another of the great problems in America today. To give hypnotic suggestion in the form of supportive therapy is not a cure for the escape tendencies that cause alcoholism, but it is sometimes possible to reroute the symptom into channels which are less socially objectionable and less destructive to the organism.

TERMINOLOGY

The authors of this book subscribe to no one "school" of psychology or psychotherapy, preferring the eclectic approach. However, it has been found necessary to use some standard terminology in presenting the idea of the multiple functions of the human mind. For that purpose we have used several popular, although somewhat controversial, dichotomies as follows:

Cortical activity .... Thalamic activity
Will .... Imagination
Conscious mind .... Unconscious mind
Intellect .... Emotion
Thinking .... Feeling

While realizing that these concepts are far from accurate in a scientific sense, we have found them useful in the necessarily brief introduction to hypnotic phenomena which must be given to most patients.

It may be helpful to explain to the patient that the "conscious" mind and the "unconscious" mind do not exist as real entities. They are constructs, labels that are somewhat descriptive, and are not to be taken literally.

The word "sleep," as used in hypnotic technique, is also somewhat confusing. This word is used partly because of its traditional background, and partly because it carries connotations of "eyes closed," "body relaxed," "nothing can disturb you." The sound of the word is also soporific. In work on patients, particularly on insomnia cases, when giving suggestions to insure a good night's rest, the word "slumber" can be used to denote natural sleep as distinguished from hypnotic "sleep."

THE AUTHORS

In order that the reader may distinguish between the two authors of this work, it should be mentioned that Charles Edward Cooke is a practicing psychologist who has, in classes, taught the techniques of hypnosis to physicians in general practice, dentists, psychologists, and psychiatrists. A. E. Van Vogt is a professional writer.

HISTORY OMITTED

The authors have deliberately omitted historical material except for casual references, feeling that there are already in existence many fine works covering this phase of hypnosis. Those interested in the history and the more theoretical aspects of hypnosis will find an adequate guide to such reading in the bibliography.

CHAPTER I

THE FIRST INTERVIEW

Mrs. J. entered the consultation room of the psychologist displaying obvious nervousness. She seated herself tensely on the edge of her chair, and the following conversation took place:

Mrs. J.: "Dr. X told me that you could help me by hypnotizing me."

Psychologist: "That is possible. Would you care to tell me a little more about it?"

A ten minute discussion of her symptoms then took place.

Psychologist: "And now tell me, how do you feel about being hypnotized?"

Mrs. J.: (nervously) "To tell the truth, I'm afraid. But I need help so much that *I will try just as hard as I can.*"

Psychologist: "Why are you afraid?"

Mrs. J. "I've always been afraid of losing consciousness. When I had my operation, I fought the ether so hard they had to hold me. Besides, I don't like the idea of anyone overcoming my will power. I'm a little afraid of what might happen while I'm unconscious. What if I didn't wake up?"

Psychologist: "Perhaps we'd better talk a little about hypnosis. Have you ever seen anyone hypnotized?"

Mrs. J.: "When I was a little girl, a hypnotist came to

1

our town to give a show. He put a woman to sleep in a furniture store window, and kept her there for three days. I used to go down, but I was almost afraid to look at her. I went to the show in the end, but I was afraid to look directly at the hypnotist. A friend of my mother's said that if you didn't look at him, he couldn't 'get you.' Several boys that I knew went up on the stage, and they had to do everything he told them to."

Psychologist: "We will have to correct some of your ideas. In the first place, when you're hypnotized you don't go to sleep the way you do at night. It's more like the dreamy relaxed, drowsy feeling that you may have on a vacation morning when you awaken at your usual time and then realize that you don't have to get up. You snuggle back into the bed and enjoy a sensation of well-being. You hear the birds outside and other noises, but they don't mean very much to you. Perhaps you smell the bacon frying and the coffee cooking in the kitchen, but for the moment you simply relax in peace and contentment. That sounds all right so far, doesn't it?"

Mrs. J.: "It seems all right."

Psychologist: "What I've just told you is a fairly exact description of the feeling you'll have when you are hypnotized. You *never* lose consciousness. You are always aware of the words being spoken by the person who has hypnotized you, and frequently you hear the other things that go on around you, such as an automobile outside, someone typing in the next room, or hard heels on the sidewalk outside. Although you may hear these things, they don't matter. It's beginning to sound more normal, isn't it?"

2

Mrs. J. "Yes, if that's the way it is——"

Psychologist: "You never lose consciousness with hypnosis. If you do lose consciousness it will be because you have actually gone to sleep and are taking a nap. In that case, you would not hear what I was saying, nor would you do anything that I asked you to do. And when your nap was finished, you would awaken just as you would from any nap. That is what would happen if I hypnotized you deeply and then left you. Without my voice to keep you from passing out of the hypnotic state, you would either awaken, or would take a nap and awaken when you were slept out. No one could ever keep you hypnotized like the woman in the show window unless you'd had lots of practice and a definite reason for putting on such an act. Don't forget, that girl made her living by being a hypnotic subject. That makes the whole incident more understandable, doesn't it?"

Mrs. J.: "Yes, it does. I never thought of that."

Psychologist: "Being hypnotized is not like taking ether. As for your will power, that has nothing to do with being hypnotized. It's not a matter of will power, it has to do with the the imagination. When you're hypnotized, you do not stop thinking. Your thinking merely slows down, and you permit your imagination to be guided by the hypnotist. Now let me show you what I mean *without* hypnosis. Will you please sit back in the chair, and make yourself as comfortable as you can. Now place your right elbow on the arm of the chair, and then let your arm relax with the hand out in space. Now, please clench your fist. That's right. Now, bring your fist up to your shoulder. That was a conscious

3

action, wasn't it? You clenched your fist and raised your arm consciously and purposely, because I asked you to do it. I'm going to hold your hand down now while you do it again. I'll offer enough resistance, so that you will have to work hard in bringing your hand to your shoulder. You will feel the pull in the various muscles involved. All right, I'm taking hold. So please bring your arm up again. Bring it right on up. I'm making it hard for you, but you can do it. You can feel the pull in the muscles, can't you?"

Mrs. J.: "Oh, yes, I can feel the muscles straining."

Psychologist: "But you're doing this consciously, aren't you?

Mrs. J.: "Of course."

Psychologist: "Now, relax your arm again, but keep the fist clenched. Don't pay any attention to me. Please look out the window. Watch the traffic go by. Listen to the birds out there. Whatever you can hear, get interested in and don't *pay any attention to me.* I am going to talk to your hand and arm. Now, HAND, come up to the shoulder just the way you did before, but this time without any effort on Mrs. J.'s part. MUSCLES, contract just the way you did before when Mrs. J. was pulling and I was holding the hand down. HAND, come up ... up ... up ... up ...

"You keep your attention outside the window, Mrs. J. Don't pay any attention to what your hand and I are doing here. Come on up, HAND, up ... up ... up ... MUSCLES, contract ... contract ... contract ... contract ... "

The psychologist kept talking this way for several minutes, particularly repeating the words "up" and "contract." At first there was no motion of the hand, but

4

after a while the muscles did start to contract, and the hand began to move up to the shoulder. At first there were a few slight jerky movements, and then the contraction of the muscles became more noticeable. When the hand had moved up several inches, Mrs. J. began to smile, and found it hard to keep her attention away from the hand. Finally, she turned her head to look at it. The arm relaxed immediately.

Mrs. J.: "That was a most peculiar feeling. I didn't think my hand would come up, because at first nothing happened. Then I began to feel funny little tugs in my muscles. When the hand did come up, I certainly didn't have anything to do with it."

Psychologist: "Yes, you did, Mrs. J. But it was the 'unconscious' part of you that did it. When you kept your 'thinking' and 'will power' occupied by concentrating your interest on what was going on outside, I was able to guide your imagination, or your 'unconscious' mind. Your muscles responded to your imagination. You were fully conscious of everything that happened, weren't you?"

Mrs. J.: "Oh, yes, I knew everything."

Psychologist: "But as soon as you brought your will power back to the arm, it pushed your imagination out of the way, and your arm relaxed, didn't it?"

Mrs. J.: "That's right. As soon as I really thought about my arm, it didn't act that way any more."

Psychologist: "Mrs. J., that is a very small sample of what hypnosis is like. You were really slightly hypnotized while your arm was coming up. I didn't tell you that you would be hypnotized because of your unjustified fear of it. But it's true. You have already experienced a light stage of hypnosis. You can see for yourself that it has nothing to do with your will power or losing conscious-

ness, or 'going to sleep' or 'loss of control,' and it
certainly can't be compared to taking ether. As
for your original intention of 'trying just as hard
as you can,' that would be the worst thing possible.
Because when you 'try,' you are using your 'will
power,' and that prevents the effective use of the
imagination. Now, do you think you would like
to practice a little more hypnotic response? This
time we could help you feel extremely comfortable,
so that when you leave here you'll have a wonderful sensation of being refreshed.

"There are many ways of helping you to get
hypnotized, or—and this may interest you—of hypnotizing yourself. It can be done. In fact, no
hypnotist ever really hypnotizes anyone else. It
may appear as if he does. You may think you are
seeing him do it. But in every case, all the hypnotist does is to *guide* the subject's imagination. He
establishes a pattern. He shows the subject how
to handle himself. Of course if the subject, because
of false understanding of what was happening,
believed that he had to do what the hypnotist
asked him to do, then he would have to—though
even that is not always so. However *that belief*
would be responsible, and *not* the hypnotic situation.

"There are many waking states, where belief
plays much the same role. A stenographer, for
instance, believes that she has to take dictation
from her boss. So when he sounds the buzzer, she
drops whatever else she is doing and goes in to
take down his words. Of course, she is paid to do
that, but it's her acceptance of her position that is
important. If her boss asked her to scrub the floor,
the suggestion would probably not be so acceptable.
That's a good comparison, because it shows a per-

6

son who is doing what she believes she ought to do and refusing to do what she doesn't believe should be expected of her. Some people do things because they believe the person who pays their salary has a right to expect it. Other people do things because they love somebody. Whatever their motivation, when you get down into it, you'll find there is a belief involved.

"Hypnosis is like that also. By this time you probably understand that you don't *have* to do anything I tell you. To that extent, so far as hypnosis is concerned, your belief has changed.

"Now, let's clear up another misunderstanding. The hypnotist often talks about sleep, when he knows that you are not going to sleep at all in the usual sense of the word. The reason he talks about it is because the word "sleep" reminds us of certain other things besides unconsciousness. It also means body relaxed, eyes closed, not paying much attention to what happens outside, having dreams —and the last is the most important because being profoundly hypnotized is very much like having a dream, a pleasant dream.

"So you see, when I say 'sleep!' I am using a word that means all these other things, and has nothing to do with unconsciousness. Under these circumstances you will be able to accept it, won't you? Would you like to try it now?"

Mrs. J.: "Yes, I would like to try it. When I get hypnotized, will you be able to tell me that all of my troubles are gone, and will they be gone?"

Psychologist: "I am sorry to disappoint you, Mrs. J., but hypnosis is not a magic wand. It is simply a condition of the mind in which you are able to learn new things much more rapidly than you ordinarily could, and in which you can unlearn some things which you believe implicitly but which *are not so*. Many of our troubles are caused by knowledge which is simply not true. You may not understand exactly what I mean without an illustration, so tell me: When you were a child, did you believe in Santa Claus?"

Mrs. J.: "Of course. When I was seven, my girl friend told me that there was no Santa Claus, and I was heartbroken."

Psychologist: "You really believed in Santa Claus then, and you had good reason to believe in him. First of all, your parents told you there was a Santa Claus. Second, every Christmas there was tangible evidence of the fact that Santa Claus existed. You got presents 'from Santa Claus.' Third, it was such a nice idea that once you formed it you wanted to hold it. You hated to lose the idea, and yet it wasn't really so. You *knew* that there was a Santa Claus, but your knowing it didn't make it so in reality. You *knew* something that wasn't so, didn't you?"

Mrs. J.: "Yes, I guess I did."

Psychologist: "When you came in here, you *knew* quite a few things about hypnosis that were not so, didn't you?"

Mrs. J.: "Yes, I guess I had the wrong idea."

Psychologist: "Sometimes, these wrong ideas require quite a little reeducation. Hypnosis speeds that up. If I had merely told you that you had nothing to fear, you wouldn't have believed me, would you?"

Mrs. J.: "I was pretty scared."

Psychologist: "How do you feel now? Would you like to have another hypnotic experience?"

8

Mrs. J.: "Yes, I would. But if you can't tell my troubles to go away, what good is it going to do me?"

Psychologist: "First, we'll teach you how to relax completely, how to achieve a more thorough relaxation than you have enjoyed since childhood. Second, we may be able to produce quick changes in some of your more simple problems. For instance, when you are deeply hypnotized, I'll give you a suggestion that you will go to sleep tonight, and will sleep continuously all night long. That is a simple suggestion that may take care of just one of your troubles. But we can frequently handle it. As for the rest, we'll have to study the details of your problem, and solve different aspects of it in different ways. You must realize that 'unhappiness' or 'emotional difficulties' or 'psychosomatic disturbances' never exist alone and by themselves. There are always a number of factors, some of which are obvious to you. There are the symptoms which sent you to the doctor and ultimately brought you here. There are probably other symptoms which you have not recognized as such because to you they are your normal and usual way of life. For example, we haven't even mentioned your social relations. Do you and your husband have lots of friends, and mix in the social affairs of your community?"

Mrs. J.: "We used to, but recently we've stayed at home all the time. We never seem to go any place. And most of our friends have stopped coming over."

Psychologist: "Could that possibly have any relationship to your insomnia and to the other matters we spoke of?"

Mrs. J.: "I hadn't thought of it, but perhaps it could."

9

Psychologist: "We can explore those things later. Our first step is to teach you to get hypnotized. We'll spend a little time on it. In the beginning we'll work on simple little things, like having your arm lift up by itself, or having your eyelids stick so tightly closed that when you try to open them with 'will power,' your imagination will hold them closed and you won't be able to open them. These tests, and other tests which I will explain to you, might be compared to learning the scales and doing finger exercises if you were taking piano lessons. Playing the scales is not music. Finger exercises are not music. Every piano player wants to play beautiful concertos, or red hot jive, but before he can do these things, he has to master the basic steps. In the same way, the simple exercises will teach you a new way of using your nervous system. When you have learned that way, we can use the new method to solve your problems rapidly.

"These little tests are also useful to me. I cannot tell by looking at you whether you are lightly or profoundly hypnotized. I can tell by giving you the tests. At a light level of hypnosis, some tests will work and some will not. As you go deeper, more and more will work. When you have learned to respond profoundly, almost all of them will work. If you fail to respond to any one particular test, *it makes no difference*. It is like hitting a false note on the piano the first time you play a piece. You simply do it over and over till you can do it right. Now, if you're ready we'll go to work."

Mrs. J.: "I'm ready."

Psychologist: "All right, remember *not* to try hard. Just let things happen."

At this point, the psychologist started into the technique of Chapter II.

The foregoing interview, while wholly fictitious, is typical of many first interviews in the office of psychologists or counselors who use hypnosis.

CHAPTER II

WORDS THAT WORK

A Visual Fixation Technique
For Inducing an "Educational" Hypnosis

Visual fixation is one of the oldest and most effective methods of hypnotizing. The wording that follows is for use with a spiral. Any other object, such as a flickering or fixed light, a nailhead, or a spot on the wall, or the reflection of highlights on a shiny surface can be used. In that case, substitute the name of your fixation object for the word *(spiral)* which is in italics for easy identification.

PREPARATORY SUGGESTIONS

Dots (. . .) indicate a pause. Other reading instructions will be given where used.

1. **Relax comfortably in your seat . . . Please place your feet flat on the floor . . . Move back firmly against the back of the chair . . . Unclasp your hands and let them lie loosely on your thighs . . . Relax your hands and arms.**

Observe the manner in which the subject does what you ask. You are already getting response to suggestion. Make sure that you are understood. If the subject understands but does not do what you ask, question him. He is resisting consciously or unconsciously. Analyze the reason.

2. **The** *spiral* **at which you are looking is simply an object upon which you can closely fix your attention. Please fix your attention upon it . . . While you are looking at it you will not be distracted by other things. Keep your attention firmly fixed on it. As you watch it you will find your eyes going slightly out of focus. Let them go. Let the** *spiral* **soften**

and flow ... Just watch it ... Watch the center of it .. Make believe that I am talking to someone else. You hear me vaguely but your ATTENTION IS ON THE *SPIRAL*.

3. Please be assured that nothing will be done to embarrass you or cause you any discomfort. Quite the contrary, if you have the ability to focus your attention closely, and to accept in a passive manner the suggestions that I am reading to you, the following experience will be one of the most refreshing and delightful of your whole life.

4. As you watch the *spiral* you will notice that your eyes become drowsy, drowsy and sleepy, very sleepy. Soon they will close of their own accord as your body relaxes more and more. Soon your eyes will close.

If the subject's eyes close before they are TOLD to close, finish the paragraph that you are reading and turn immediately to paragraph 16. Look at the subject frequently, at least at the end of each paragraph. Watch his eyes for signs of heaviness.

5. Your ability to be hypnotized has absolutely nothing to do with your intelligence or your strength of will. It depends entirely on your ability to focus your attention closely and to keep it focused without wandering. You are finding it easy to do this with the aid of the *spiral*.

LULLABY

Read the following monotonously. Make no effort to read in an "interesting" or dramatic fashion. Make your voice as level and even as a metronome. Emphasize each syllable equally. This is a "lullaby."

6. Let us now relax every muscle in the body ... Relax the toes on your right foot. Let them go limp, limp, heavy and relaxed. Let this relaxation creep up through the ball ... and the arch of the foot ... all the way to the ankle ... so that your right foot is completely relaxed, relaxed and heavy, heavy and limp.

13

7. Now relax the toes on the left foot, the toes, the ball, the arch and the heel. Your left foot is completely relaxed, relaxed and limp, limp and heavy. Both feet are now completely relaxed, completely relaxed, relaxed and heavy.

8. Let this heaviness creep up the calf of your right leg . . . so that you are now completely relaxed from the tip of your right toes to the knee. Now let the left calf relax in the same manner so that both feet and legs are completely relaxed up to the knees.

9. Let the relaxation extend up through the large muscles of the right thigh so that your right leg is completely relaxed up to the hip. Now let the left thigh also relax so that your feet and legs are heavy, heavy and relaxed, heavy and relaxed, relaxed and limp. So relaxed, so limp, so heavy.

10. Your eyes are very, very heavy now, so drowsy and so sleepy. It is becoming difficult for you to keep your eyes open. Soon they will become so relaxed and so sleepy that they will close of their own accord. Soon your eyes will close of their own accord. They are becoming so drowsy and so sleepy with the watching . . . watching . . . watching.

Observe the reaction of the subject to the words "relaxing" and "relaxation." The chief complaint of some people is that "they just can't relax." In such cases use another technique or substitute the words "lazy," "comfortable," "loose," "limp," etc.

11. Now relax the fingers of the right hand. Feel them getting limp and heavy and relaxed. Feel the right hand relaxing more and more. Getting more and more limp, more and more heavy. Now the fingers of the left hand are letting go completely, all the muscles relaxing, the fingers getting heavy, limp, relaxed. The left hand becoming relaxed and heavy. Now let that feeling flow up the arms, the right forearm relaxed, the left forearm relaxed, the right upper arm relaxed, the left upper arm relaxed, both hands, both arms relaxed and heavy, relaxed and heavy and limp, all the way up to

14

the shoulders. By this time you probably notice a slight, pleasant tingling in the toes and fingers. This feeling will increase until you are completely bathed in a pleasant glow of utter relaxation.

12. Now we are going to relax the body. The hips, the large back muscles, the abdomen, the chest muscles and the shoulders will all relax at once. We are going to take three deep breaths. Each time we exhale we will notice the body relaxing more and more. With the third deep breath will come a complete and utter relaxation of the entire body. Now breathe slowly in . . . in . . . in, a full deep breath. Out! Relax completely. Now a deeper breath in . . . in . . . in . . . in . . . in. Out, and relax completely. Now, the last time, in . . . in . . . in. . . . in . . . in. Out and completely relaxed. Now you are breathing slowly, gently, deeply as a sleeper breathes. Every muscle in your chest, shoulders, back, abdomen and hips is completely relaxed and your whole body is heavy, heavy, heavy and limp.

13. You are now completely relaxed. your arms are relaxed, your legs are relaxed, your body is relaxed. Your eyes are so sleepy, so drowsy. The lids are so heavy. All the muscles in your neck are now beginning to relax. Your head feels so heavy as the muscles release their tension. Let your jaw muscles relax so that your teeth do not quite touch . . . Jaw muscles are completely relaxed. Let all the muscles of the face and scalp relax completely. So limp, so heavy, so completely relaxed.

14. Now we are going to relax the eye muscles. I am going to start counting. On the first count close your eyes. On the second count open them with your attention still focused on the *spiral*. On the third count close them and on the fourth count open them. Continue in this manner. Each time your eyes open have your attention fixed closely on the *spiral*. You will find that each time you close your eyes they will want to stay closed. Each time you open them it will be

more difficult to do so, more difficult than the last time, much more difficult. Soon your eyelids will stick so tightly closed that it will be impossible to open them. Soon they will stay closed.

15. One, close your eyes, ... two, open ... three, closed and heavy ... four, open ... five, closed and so sleepy ... six, sleepy ... seven, so very sleepy, peaceful and relaxed .. eight, sleepy ... nine, so sleepy, so sleepy, so sleepy ... ten, sleepy ... eleven, so completely and utterly relaxed, feeling so peaceful and calm, so free from tension ... twelve, sleepy ... thirteen, drowsy and peaceful, completely relaxed, every muscle free from tension ... fourteen, so sleepy ... fifteen, so sleepy, so sleepy, so sleepy, so sleepy ... sixteen, so sleepy ... seventeen, feeling so comfortable, so perfectly relaxed, so peaceful and restful, peaceful and restful ... eighteen, so sleepy ... nineteen, relaxed and calm, relaxed and calm, so dreamy, so drowsy, so sleepy ... twenty, so sleepy ... twenty-one, drowsy and relaxed, peaceful and calm, peaceful and comfortable ... twenty-two, sleepy ... twenty-three, drowsy and dreamy ... twenty-four, sleepy ... twenty-five, so sleepy ... twenty-six, sleepy ... twenty-seven, sleepy ... twenty-eight ... twenty-nine, sleepy ... thirty.

Increase the tempo of the count gradually until the subject finds it impossible to keep up with the count. If the eyes remain closed after a brief or prolonged count, continue counting for a few numbers and then proceed with paragraph 16. If he continues to open his eyes after counting to 100, ask him to close them and leave them closed.

... thirty-one ... thirty-two ... thirty-three ... thirty-four ... thirty-five ... thirty-six ... thirty-seven ... thirty-eight ... thirty-nine ... forty ... forty-one ... forty-two ... etc.

Count continuously without missing a number but keep increasing the tempo.

... fifty-five ... fifty-six ... fifty-seven ... etc ... sixty-seven, sixty-eight, sixty-nine ... etc ... eighty-one, eighty-two, eighty-three, eighty-four ... etc ... ninety-nine, one-

16

hundred. Just rest with your eyes closed. Let them stay closed and relax more and more, more and more. You are slipping into a deep, sound, hypnotic sleep. You are going deeper and deeper to sleep, deeper and deeper to sleep. Deeper and deeper, deeper and deeper, deeper and deeper, deeper and deeper.

PRECAUTIONARY SUGGESTIONS

16. You are slipping into a deep hypnotic sleep, a hypnotic sleep, a hypnotic sleep. You hear every word that I say, and yet you are sound asleep, sound asleep, sound asleep. You are feeling so good, so perfectly relaxed, so peaceful and calm, relaxed and calm, peaceful and comfortable, very comfortable. You hear every word that I say. You will continue to hear every word that I say, and yet you are sound asleep, sound asleep, sound asleep. You are sinking deeper and deeper, deeper and deeper, deeper and deeper, down, down, down down, down, deeper and deeper. Please stay asleep until I ask you to wake up. Your acceptance of the ideas you are about to receive will make this the most pleasant experience of your life. You want this to be a wonderful experience. You want me to help you with these ideas, so stay asleep until I ask you to wake up. Stay asleep until I ask you to awaken. Your deep, sound, restful sleep will continue until I awaken you.

Gradually change from the monotone of the "lullaby" to a brisk, business-like voice. Make this transition smoothly. Be firm without dominating. When a word is CAPITAL-IZED, emphasize it forcefully.

17. You now have the opportunity to experience the power of your own "unconscious mind." We are going to measure your ability to accept a suggestion, to make it YOUR OWN and to implant it firmly in YOUR unconscious mind. When you later consciously try to oppose the suggestion you find yourself unable to do so. I am going to describe each suggestion before asking you to accept it. You may refuse any

17

suggestion at your pleasure, but if you ACCEPT a suggestion you find yourself COMPLETELY RESPONSIVE to it. You may show that you accept a suggestion by nodding your head. You can nod your head easily and without awakening. Do you understand me clearly? If so, please nod your head ... If you do not understand me, shake your head.

Wait for an acknowledgment. If the head is nodded, proceed. If the head is shaken, repeat paragraph 17, and if the head is not nodded at the end of the second reading, go through it again, sentence by sentence. Ask for a nod to indicate understanding at the end of each sentence. When you find the point of misunderstanding, discuss this point "ad lib" until you do get a nod of understanding.

18. If for any reason you do not wish to accept a suggestion, shake your head. Do you understand?

Wait for a nod.

EYE CATALEPSY

19. That's fine. Our first test will be to lock your eyelids so tightly closed that no conscious effort that you can make will open them. Are you willing to do this?

Wait for a nod.

20. Very well, your eyelids are very, very heavy. They are locked closed, tightly closed.

Wait. Watch the eyes for evidence of response.

Locking tighter, AND TIGHTER, and TIGHTER. THEY ARE SEALED TOGETHER. YOUR EYELIDS ARE LOCKED TOGETHER. THEY ARE LOCKED SO TIGHT THAT NO MATTER HOW HARD YOU TRY TO OPEN THEM THEY CANNOT OPEN. THEY SIMPLY LOCK TIGHTER AND TIGHTER AND TIGHTER. THE HARDER YOU TRY TO OPEN THEM THE TIGHTER THEY LOCK. Try to open them, but IT IS ABSOLUTELY IMPOSSIBLE. THEY WILL NOT OPEN. Go ahead and try, THEY WILL NOT OPEN.

Watch subject. After he has made a futile effort, or after a five second wait during which no attempt is made, continue.

21. All right, don't try any more. Relax completely. When we release the eyes, please keep them closed. NOW YOUR EYES ARE NO LONGER LOCKED TIGHTLY CLOSED. You can open them easily when I ask you to, but LEAVE THEM CLOSED for the present. Relax even more and go deeper and deeper to sleep, deeper and deeper to sleep, deeper and deeper to sleep, deeper and deeper, deeper and deeper, deeper and deeper.

If the subject succeeded in forcing his eyes open, he was not quite deep enough for this test. Retain your composure. Say to him, "All right, you were not quite deep enough for this one, but you soon will be. Please close your eyes." Reread paragraph 16, then start reading paragraph 29. When the hand levitation has been achieved, the eye catalepsy will almost invariably work. Return to it and work through the other tests.

HEAVY ARM CATALEPSY

22. Our next test will be to make your right arm so heavy that you cannot lift it. If you wish to do this, nod your head.

Wait for acknowledgement. If the subject shakes his head, indicating a refusal of any particular suggestion, say, "Very well, we will pass this one." And go on to the next test.

IMPORTANT: If at any time during the hypnosis the subject awakens spontaneously, the operator has two choices. (1) Ask him to close his eyes and again relax. Talk "deeper and deeper" for a minute or so. In most cases this is sufficient to reestablish hypnosis with a depth equal or greater than that attained in the previous trance. (2) Say to the subject, "WAKE UP! YOU ARE WIDE AWAKE!" Take this precaution even though the subject is obviously and apparently awake because the awakening signal becomes associated in his mind with the experience of "awakening." There is also the possibility that the subject is in a much deeper trance than you suspect, and has simply opened his eyes while remaining in hypnosis.

23. That is fine. Now relax more and more, every muscle in your body completely relaxed, relaxed and heavy. Your right arm especially relaxed, heavy and relaxed. Every fiber of every muscle in your right hand, your right arm, and your right shoulder is completely relaxed. That makes your hand and arm feel VERY HEAVY, VERY HEAVY.

Subject's hands are resting loosely on his thighs. Gently push the relaxed arm to the outside so that it will fall and hang straight down, or in an armchair, fall to the cushion. Observe the degree of relaxation. If the subject *lowers* his arm rather than permitting it to *fall*, put the arm back and talk relaxation until the arm falls loosely.

24. See how heavy it feels? Your hand is getting heavier and heavier, HEAVIER AND HEAVIER, HEAVIER AND HEAVIER, HEAVIER AND HEAVIER, MUCH TOO HEAVY TO LIFT. YOUR ARM IS GETTING HEAVIER AND HEAVIER, HEAVIER AND HEAVIER. YOUR HAND IS SO HEAVY THAT YOU CANNOT LIFT IT. YOU CANNOT LIFT YOUR HAND. IT IS MUCH TOO HEAVY TO LIFT, MUCH TOO HEAVY. IT FEELS AS THOUGH IT WERE MADE OF SOLID LEAD, SOLID LEAD, FAR TOO HEAVY TO LIFT. Try to lift it. IT IS MUCH TOO HEAVY TO LIFT.

WAIT A FEW SECONDS. If the arm lifts an inch or so, and the struggle to lift it is apparent, but unsuccessful, ignore it. If the arm lifts six or eight inches and is held there, say "IT IS GETTING HEAVIER AND HEAVIER, THE WEIGHT IS DRAGGING IT DOWN, DOWN, DOWN." Repeat this several times. If the arm drops down, you may regard it as a successful test. If not, reassure the subject that although HE failed this test, he will probably succeed on the next one.

25. **Don't struggle to lift it any more. You see, at this time your "unconscious mind" is far more powerful than any conscious effort you can make. If you accept a suggestion it is COMPLETELY EFFECTIVE. Now your arm is getting lighter and lighter. Now it is completely normal and relaxed, light and normal. You may move it easily if you wish to. Will you please put it back in your lap? It moves easily now. Go deeper and deeper to sleep.**

Observe the ease with which the subject retuns the hand to the lap. *This is important.* Be sure that all suggestion of heaviness is eliminated. If necessary, continue with suggestions of "completely normal." Whenever a test suggestion is *not* to carry over into the waking state as a post-hypnotic suggestion, it should be completely neutralized.

RIGID ARM CATALEPSY

26. **Our next test will be to make your left arm so rigid that you cannot bend it. If you wish to do this, please lift your left arm, extend it straight out from the shoulder and clench the fist.**

Wait for the subject to show, by extending his arm, that he is willing. If he extends it with the elbow bent, ask him to straighten the arm. If he does not extend it, ask him, "Do you understand? If you understand, please nod your head." If he understands but does not wish to do it, say, "Please shake your head if you do not wish to do this one." Then pass to the next test.

27. **That's right. Now you notice all the muscles in your left arm beginning to get tense and rigid. You can feel the muscles tightening up...tightening up... tighter and tighter. You can feel your whole arm getting rigid... rigid... rigid ... STIFF AND UNYIELDING ... RIGID AS A BAR OF STEEL. EVERY MUSCLE IN YOUR ARM IS RIGID.**

21

YOUR ARM IS NOW SO RIGID THAT NOTHING CAN BEND IT. NOTHING CAN BEND IT. RIGID AS A BAR OF STEEL. YOUR ARM CANNOT BE BENT. Try and bend it. IT WILL NOT BEND. Try to bend it. IT WILL NOT BEND. Try to bend it. IT IS AS RIGID AS STEEL.

Wait a few seconds. If the subject's arm starts to bend, though with obvious effort, keep saying, "RIGID, RIGID AS STEEL, STIFF AND RIGID." From this point on, if any particular test fails, dismiss it casually. Indicate that though he failed in this one he will succeed with the next. Do not be afraid to challenge on any test. A test is effective only if both you and the subject are satisfied that a definite response is obtained. However, a test may be satisfactory even if the subject meets the challenge. The measure of success is the *difficulty* with which the arm is bent. A subject who bends his arm, but with great effort, should have the difficulty pointed out to him as evidence of a successful response. Remember that a failure is *not* a failure on your part, but a failure on the part of the subject. Practice can make a good subject out of a poor one.

28. You see, it will not bend. Now the muscles are relaxing, relaxing, relaxing. The tension is leaving your arm. Now you can bend it. It feels fine, marvelous. You may put it in your lap, will you, please?

HAND LEVITATION

29. So far we have been demonstrating how your "unconscious mind" can prevent you from consciously doing things. Now we can demonstrate the power of the "unconscious mind" to DO something without any conscious effort from you. This test will be to have your hand lift from your lap without any effort on your part. If you would like to feel this, nod your head.

Wait for acknowledgment.

30. First of all we want to know what muscles are used in

22

this movement, so will you please bend your right elbow and raise your right hand ... touch the shoulder ... that's right. Now put your hand back in your lap. We have a muscle pattern now. Will you please do it again? That's right. Now put it back in your lap ... and again bring it up to your shoulder ... and put it back in your lap.

31. Now make ABSOLUTELY no effort to raise your hand. We are going to turn THAT job over to your "unconscious mind." Leave your arm as relaxed as the other arm which has not moved. An interesting thing will soon happen. The SAME muscles that tightened up a few seconds ago are again starting to contract. The muscles are contracting and lifting your hand up ... up ... up. The feeling is strange. Your hand seems to get lighter ... and lighter ... and lighter ... and finally floats up of its own accord. Your hand is floating up ... up ... up ... up ... up ... up ... up ... up ... up ... up ... up ... up. Your hand is getting lighter and lighter, lighter and lighter, floating, floating, floating ... up ... up ... up.

Use a "lullaby technique" here ... steady tempo and level pitch of voice. This test usually takes several minutes, in some cases fifteen or twenty minutes. Continue alternating the last two sentences of paragraph 31. If after ten minutes the hand has not moved noticeably, gently place your fingers under the wrist and lift the hand up two or three inches so that it is free of all support and read paragraph 31A.

(31A. You don't seem to have quite enough power to get   )
(started. Just hold your hand THERE. Don't make any   )
(effort to lift it or to resist, just hold it there. Up ... up   )
(... up ... etc., lighter and lighter, etc.   )

In ten minutes more the hand will have raised noticeably or the subject will have relaxed the arm and dropped it to the original position. In the latter case, abandon this test. If there has been a definite and noticeable motion, but you do not wish to take the time to complete it, lift the subject's hand to touch his shoulder.

32. Up...up...up...up...up...higher and higher, higher and higher, your hand is moving toward your shoulder. Now it is touching your shoulder... now your arm is relaxing ...it feels FINE, WONDERFUL, PERFECT IN EVERY WAY. You may move it as you wish.

AUTOMATIC MOTION

33. Now we can demonstrate how the "unconscious mind" can keep you doing something even against your strongest effort to stop. Would you like to see how this works? If you would, just nod your head. Nod your head.

Wait for the acknowledgment.

34. That's fine. Please raise the hand with which you write. Put it up in front of you. Now imagine that you are back in school standing at the blackboard with chalk in your hand. You are about to practice making ovals. You remember the ovals? Please start making ovals. Round and round. Round and round. That's right. Remember how you used to make them? Round and round, round and round. Keep on making the ovals, round and round. So far you are doing this because I asked you to and because you want to, but we are going to turn this motion over to your "unconscious mind."

35. As you continue to make the ovals round and round, the action is becoming just as automatic as the beating of your heart. As you know, the action of your heart is not subject to your control. Your heart speeds up and slows down in response to the needs of your body in a completely unconscious way. THINKING about it will not change its action. It is AUTOMATIC, beyond your control. YOU CANNOT STOP YOUR HEART from beating by thinking about it.

36. In the same way the motion of your hand is now completely automatic. THE MOTION OF YOUR HAND IS JUST AS AUTOMATIC AS THE BEATING OF YOUR

HEART. IT IS NOW IMPOSSIBLE FOR YOU TO STOP MAKING OVALS. YOUR UNCONSCIOUS MIND IS FORCING YOUR HAND TO GO ROUND AND ROUND, ROUND AND ROUND, IN SPITE OF ANY EFFORT YOU MAY MAKE TO STOP IT. Try to stop it. IT WILL NOT STOP. Try hard to stop it. YOUR HAND KEEPS GOING ROUND AND ROUND, ROUND AND ROUND.

Pause for the test. As soon as the subject has made an obvious effort to stop the motion, continue. If the motion slows down, but does not stop, continue saying, "ROUND AND ROUND, ROUND AND ROUND" until the subject stops fighting it. If the subject simply relaxes the arm and stops the motion, the test has failed. Admit it as a failure *on the part of the subject* and continue.

37. Now the motion is slowing down, slowing down. Now your conscious control has returned. Now your arm is relaxed and you may do with it as you wish. Relax completely and go deeper and deeper to sleep. Deeper and deeper to sleep. Far deeper than you have been before.

CONDITIONING FOR FUTURE RESPONSE

The following suggestions will make future hypnosis, on the part of the subject, easier and faster. It also gives the subject reassurance, which is invaluable.

38. The next time you wish to be hypnotized you will find it much easier. You will go much deeper, very much faster. NO ONE WILL EVER BE ABLE TO HYPNOTIZE YOU UNLESS YOU GIVE YOUR VERBAL PERMISSION. IN ORDER TO BE HYPNOTIZED IT IS NECESSARY FOR YOU TO SAY ALOUD THAT YOU WISH TO BE HYPNOTIZED. IF I ASK YOUR PERMISSION TO HYPNOTIZE YOU AND YOU SAY "YES," "O. K.," "SURE" OR ANY OTHER EXPRESSION OF CONSENT, YOU WILL BE HYPNOTIZED DEEPLY AND QUICKLY. IF YOU DO

NOT GIVE YOUR CONSENT, IF YOU SAY "NO" OR DO NOT SAY ANYTHING, NO ONE CAN HYPNOTIZE YOU BY ANY METHOD. If you understand, nod your head. Wait for acknowledgment. If the subject does not understand perfectly, repeat in a conversational tone, asking for a nod of understanding after each sentence. When you find the point of confusion, explain in detail.

39. The next time YOU wish to be hypnotized by ME, we can arrange a signal. We will use a signal with two parts. One part is yours and one part mine. Both parts are necessary to induce hypnosis in this way. The first part is your permission. WITHOUT YOUR PERMISSION I CAN DO NOTHING. If you give your permission I will say, "SLEEP NOW!" That is the second part. Do you understand? First your permission, second I say, "SLEEP NOW!" WITH THE WORD "NOW," YOUR EYES WILL CLOSE INSTANT-LY, WITH THE WORD "NOW," YOUR BODY WILL RELAX, WITH THE WORD "NOW," YOUR MIND WILL RELAX. WHEN I SAY "SLEEP NOW!" YOU WILL GO INTO A DEEP, DEEP SLEEP, FAR DEEPER THAN YOU ARE NOW. EVERY TIME YOU ARE HYPNOTIZED YOU ARE GOING TO GO DEEPER AND FASTER, BUT NO ONE CAN HYPNOTIZE YOU WITHOUT YOUR PERMISSION.

40. Let me repeat, if you wish to be hypnotized, SAY SO. If you say that you wish to be hypnotized, I will say "SLEEP NOW." Your eyes will close instantly. Your body will relax instantly. Your mind will relax instantly. You will go to sleep instantly. Without your permission no one can hypnotize you. Now go deeper and deeper, deeper and deeper.

POST-HYPNOTIC HANDCLASP

41. We have demonstrated various ways in which your unconscious mind can affect the activity of your body while in hypnosis. It can also have a very strong effect AFTER

you awaken and you ARE NOT HYPNOTIZED AT ALL. For example, it is possible for YOU to stick YOUR hands so tightly together that even after you awaken you will find that you cannot separate them until a signal is given. Would you like to do this one? If you would, extend your hands straight out in front of you ... palms facing each other ... now interlace your fingers ... press the palms tightly together ... press the fingers tightly against the backs of the hands.

If the subject fails to follow your lead on this one ask him to nod his head if he understands. Ask him to shake his head if he does not wish to do it. At this point you can carry on a very casual conversation with the subject without disturbing his trance in any way. If you wish him to speak to you, tell him that he can do so *without awakening*. If he objects to the post-hypnotic suggestion, do not attempt to force it. Remember that although *deeply* hypnotized, the subject is still an individual with likes and dislikes.

42.   The muscles in your fingers, your hands, your arms, are now contracting, forcing your hands tighter and tighter, tighter and tighter together. Your unconscious mind has taken complete control of your hands and arms. YOUR HANDS ARE STICKING TIGHTLY TOGETHER. THEY ARE STICKING SO TIGHTLY THAT YOU CANNOT SEPARATE THEM NO MATTER HOW HARD YOU TRY. WHEN YOU TRY TO SEPARATE THEM THEY STICK TIGHTER. THE MORE YOU TRY THE TIGHTER THEY STICK. NO FORCE ON EARTH CAN SEPARATE THEM UNTIL I TOUCH THEM AFTER YOU AWAKEN. THEY ARE STUCK TIGHTLY TOGETHER NOW AND WILL REMAIN STUCK TIGHTLY TOGETHER AFTER YOU AWAKEN UNTIL I TOUCH THEM. NOTHING CAN SEPARATE THEM UNTIL I TOUCH THEM. Now they are dropping into your lap. STUCK TIGHT TOGETHER. After you awaken, when I touch them they will relax, separate, and will FEEL PERFECT IN EVERY WAY.

When I touch them they will RELAX and FEEL PERFECT. This will occur even though you do not remember what the signal is when you awaken. Your unconscious mind will remember and your hands will respond even though you have no memory. YOU WILL BE CALM AND INTERESTED AFTER YOU AWAKEN WHEN YOU FIND THAT YOUR HANDS ARE STUCK TIGHTLY TOGETHER. YOU KNOW IT IS A TEST.

AMNESIA

43. One proof of deep hypnosis is the ability to forget what has happened. Of course you know what has happened, but it is possible for you to forget as you awaken. Just as you may find a dream at night very vivid, but forget it entirely as you awaken, you can forget what has happened since your eyes first closed. Would you like to do this? If you would, nod your head.

Wait for acknowledgment. If the subject objects to amnesia, go immediately to the awakening suggestions, paragraph 45. Tell the subject, "All right, you will remember everything when you awaken. YOUR MEMORY OF EVERY SENSATION AND TEST WILL BE PERFECT."

44. All right. You will notice that your memory is beginning to fade now. Make NO EFFORT to REMEMBER or FORGET. Make no effort at all. The memory is fading, fading, fading. Just as the memory of a dream fades away, so this memory is fading. You seem to be standing on a hill on a foggy day. The fog is rolling in, rolling in, blotting out everything. The fog is getting thicker and thicker, thicker and thicker and you are forgetting, forgetting, forgetting. The fog is so thick that you cannot see anything. You have forgotten. You have forgotten everything that happened since your eyes first closed. You have completely forgotten, completely forgotten. The fog rolled in so thick that it blotted out everything. The memory is gone, you have forgotten, forgotten,

completely forgotten, completely forgotten. The memory is buried deep in your unconscious mind. You have completely forgotten, forgotten, forgotten, forgotten, forgotten.

AWAKENING

Become enthusiastic and forceful and dramatic. "Sell" this suggestion as a radio announcer "sells" his commercial. Put pep and vigor into your voice and manner as well as the words you use.

45. When you awaken from this sleep you will be more refreshed and more invigorated than you have ever felt before in your whole life. You will ALWAYS find hypnosis relaxing, refreshing and invigorating. When you awaken from a hypnotic sleep, you awaken with the physical relaxation of a champion athlete. You are relaxed in the same way as an all-American football player is relaxed on the gridiron. Relaxed and perfectly normal, relaxed and ready for anything. Relaxed with a vigorous, dynamic relaxation that gives you pep, energy and perfect co-ordination.

46. I am going to count to three. On the count of three your eyes open. On the count of three you are wide awake. On the count of three you are alert, vital, vigorous and perfectly refreshed; refreshed as though you are awakening from a long nap. Here we go now. ONE. You are waking up now. You feel the life and energy and vigor flowing through your arms, flowing through your legs, flowing through your body. Your eyes feel fresh and clear as though they had been washed with cold spring water. From head to foot you are feeling perfect, physically perfect, mentally perfect, emotionally perfect. TWO. You are more and more awake, more and more awake, more and more awake. You feel vigorous, energetic, perfect from head to foot. You are completely refreshed, rejuvenated. Your eyes are all ready to open. You are about to wake up. THREE. WIDE AWAKE. YOU ARE WIDE AWAKE.

TESTING FOR POST-HYPNOTIC RESPONSE

This can be done quite informally. Ask the subject how he feels. Ask him to tell you what happened. Many subjects confidently state that they remember everything that happened, but are unable to mention specifically any of the tests in which they participated. Some will recall a part of what has happened. Some will be able to give you a complete, detailed account. In some the memory is completely gone.

Call the subject's attention to the condition of his hands if he has not observed it. Ask him to try to separate them. Ask him if he remembers the signal that will release them. If he has no memory, try several false signals such as standing up, taking out your handkerchief, touching his knee or shoulder, etc. After you have made these tests, touch his hands. If they do not relax immediately, tell him, "THAT'S THE SIGNAL, NOW THEY ARE COMPLETELY RELAXED."

IMPORTANT: Even if the subject shows absolutely no post-hypnotic effect, give the release signal. Sometimes post-hypnotic suggestions which appear to be ineffective have a delayed reaction.

CHAPTER III

WHAT YOU SHOULD KNOW
FOR YOUR FIRST
HYPNOSIS

Miss H. persuaded her family physician to take a course in hypnosis. She believed vaguely that therapy with hypnosis might be of benefit to her, but she refused to be hypnotized except by her own doctor. Suffering from a severe migraine headache, she accompanied him to the second lesson, and in his presence, in desperation, allowed the psychologist to hypnotize her. She was able to obtain light trance, and the headache was successfully removed —for about an hour. Again she allowed herself to be hypnotized, and once again the pain was temporarily relieved.

The experience allayed her fear of the hypnotic situation, and since her doctor did not yet feel technically capable of handling her problem, she allowed him to refer her to the psychologist for further treatment. The headache, a severe migraine case of fifteen years standing, was subsequently relieved. During the course of the treatment, the woman several times acted as subject in the classes, her purpose being to obtain deeper response. She was successful in this also, but what was done was possible only because of her gradual realization that hypnosis, far from being the dangerous experience she had anticipated, was actually safe for her. The last of the unpleasant fears vanished when she discovered that the hypnotic trance was completely in her own control. To

31

date she has been hypnotized several hundred times by about twenty-five different persons.

THE DOCTOR'S PROBLEM

Miss H. wanted to be hypnotized, and she needed merely to have her fears alleviated. Had her doctor been trained in hypnotic techniques, she would have been saved much anxiety.

In the past most doctors were not taught hypnotic techniques in medical schools. Even today little instruction is available. In these circumstances, the doctor who wishes to add hypnosis to his other techniques faces a number of minor problems.

THAT FIRST SUBJECT

Who should the first subject be? What procedure should be followed to insure that the first hypnosis is a success. Is it possible to fail so completely that there is embarrassment?

A student of hypnosis who does not practice on his family, friends, and associates is rare. Doctors frequently find their nurses willing to cooperate for this early practical experience. It is typical among students that early doubts and uncertainties are resolved after a few successful practice hypnoses. There is no reason, however, why a self-assured doctor should not attempt his first professional hypnosis immediately after glancing through the therapies and reading the first two chapters of this book. The induction technique of Chapter Two may be read to a patient who has agreed to cooperate, and there will be some response, if only in the form of a sense of relaxation.

ONE DOCTOR'S SUCCESS

One doctor of medicine with a general practice, when

trained in hypnotic technique, immediately began using hypnosis with supportive therapies. To his surprise, he had complete success in inducing hypnosis. In the first few months he did not have a single failure. Even before mastering some of the expressive therapies of more advanced psychiatry he found that hypnosis fitted in so well with his "bedside" manner that he was able to resolve almost effortlessly the doubts of his patients. In many cases this doctor found it advisable to use a disguised technique, whereby the patient did not know he was being hypnotized. As will be seen in the chapter on disguised techniques, this practice is virtually impossible to the hypnotist who is not a doctor. It lends itself, however, peculiarly to the atmosphere of the doctor's office.

DOUBTS AND FEARS
AND SUPERSTITIONS

This doctor's immediate success will probably not obtain for every doctor. In fact, success will vary from personality to personality and locality to locality. Most frequently, the temporary failure is caused by the patient's misconceptions about hypnosis. Because of this, it is well to examine briefly the nature of the doubts which are most likely to be met with in ordinary practice. What do people think when they are confronted with the suggestion that they permit themselves to be hypnotized?

MISCONCEPTION ABOUT HYPNOSIS

A good many people, even many who ought to know better, cannot escape the feeling that hypnosis is a sort of black magic having no scientific basis. Frequently this reaction is consciously denied and actually goes back to the early conditioning of the individual. Another widely prevalent belief is that only the feeble-minded, the neurotic, and the weak-willed can be hypnotized.

Practice and scientific research have proved that the higher the intelligence of the subject, the easier it is for him (or her) to respond to hypnosis. This is not surprising since hypnosis depends upon the cooperation and understanding of the subject. Actually, the difference between the two groups is only slightly in favor of the intelligent persons. Almost everyone can be hypnotized to some extent, though with some people it takes longer than with others.

FALSE FEAR
OF NOT AWAKENING

The fear of the subject that he or she will not awaken from a trance is another problem with which the hypnotist must contend. This is frequently worded in the most far-fetched manner imaginable. "Suppose, doctor, you were to die while I was in hypnosis—what would happen to me?"

It is very necessary to have an answer for this as it is one of the commonest of anxieties. The reaction of a subject to the sudden disappearance of the hypnotist would vary with "depth" of the trance and type of condition. A light trance subject can almost literally awaken at will. A patient in a somnambulistic (deep) trance would either come out of the hypnosis in a short time or go into a natural sleep and be out of the trance when he awakened from the sleep. As most people will discover when they begin to realize the possible benefits to be derived for themselves from hypnosis, the difficulty is to attain the somnambulistic state and not to get out of it.

FALSE FEAR OF DOMINATION

Ever since the publication of DuMaurier's novel about Svengali and Trilby, the fear of domination through hypnosis has titillated the imagination of the public. This fear is closely bound up with another, that the subject will be forced to do something that is contrary to his moral code. And this, in turn, is partly rooted in the unwillingness of the average individual to surrender control of his ego even for a short period of time.

Milton Erickson[10] states that the hypnotic relationship is analagous to that between physician and patient, lawyer and client, or minister and parishioner. The danger of dependency is no greater with hypnosis than without it in such a relationship.

In his book on advanced psychotherapy through hypnosis, L. R. Wolberg[36] says, "The patient will of course react to hypnosis, as he does to everything else, with his usual character strivings and defenses, but there is a coincident striving to be hypnotizable and to get on better terms with others and with himself. The hypnotic experience need not become a sop to the needs of the compulsively dependent individual. Nor will hypnosis rob a person of will power or diminish his self control. If the hypnotic experience has any effect at all, it tends to build up the patient's self-sufficiency and inner strength. This growth process, whatever its dynamic basis, has seemed to me one of the most gratifying features of hypnosis."

HYPNOTIC EXPERIENCE REASSURING

The purpose of the doctor in reassuring his patient's fears is to obtain cooperation for the first hypnosis. The subject will find the final answer to all his alarms in the process of being hypnotized. He will discover that he is *not* asleep in the usual meaning of the word, but perfectly aware of what is going on. He will take heart from the reassurance, under hypnosis, that he can never be hypnotized without his conscious and verbal consent. Possibly for the first time in his life he will experience a sense of peaceful relaxation. And then gradually he will realize that his newly gained knowledge of hypnotic technique is a protection for him against all the disguised methods of hypnotism which are consciously and unconsciously used against him every day of his life by the advertising and propaganda mediums of the press, radio, television, and billboard, the evangelical meeting, super-salesman and political spellbinder.

THE FEEL OF HYPNOSIS

The "educational" technique of Chapter II is a method of acquainting the patient with the "feel" of hypnosis. It serves no therapeutic purpose, but lays the groundwork for rapid response later. It enables the hypnotist to evaluate the "hypnotizability" of the patient and demonstrates to the patient that suggestions given in hypnosis *do* work. Seven facts are demonstrated to both hypnotist and subject:

A—Anyone who can speak and read with reasonable freedom can induce hypnosis.

B—Almost any person can respond to hypnotic suggestion to a greater or lesser degree, quickly or in a long period of training.

C—The "power" of hypnosis is a power of the person being hypnotized, NOT the "power" of the hypnotist.

D—Words have power in that they produce ideas in the minds of the listeners. The acceptance of certain ideas constitutes hypnosis.

E—Responses to identical words presented by the same person in an identical manner will vary widely from one person to another.

F—The degree of response (depth of hypnosis) can be tested by suggesting simple responses which have been studied and graded as to difficulty, corresponding to depth of hypnosis.

G—Suggestion of the "hypnotic" type plays a very great part in our everyday lives. We are constantly exposed to it. It can be used deliberately and purposefully for our physicial and emotional benefit.

Failure to respond noticeably on the first attempt is *not* a sign of abnormality. Many hours of work are sometimes needed.

Before using this technique, discuss various aspects of "hypnotism" with the patient. Be confident, but clear up misunderstandings. Speak freely in a general way about the type of tests used. Answer questions frankly. Remember that the relationship is one of cooperation. Warn the subject NOT TO TRY too hard, but be relaxed. Avoid negative suggestion. A vigorous effort to BE hypnotized will prevent a good response as much as a strong resistance.

Read all of the technique to yourself *aloud* before attempting to use it. Become familiar with the various sections which are numbered for your convenience. Learn the location and applications of the various tests. Familiarize yourself with the alternate procedures. Each section is labeled.

THE SPIRAL

Before using the induction technique of Chapter II, mount in a suitable fashion the spiral which is printed at the end of this book. Although other techniques for inducing hypnosis are available, patients frequently take for granted that a doctor will have a mechanical method. The patient, confronted with such a device in a doctor's office, expects that it will work. The spiral should be glued onto cardboard and placed on a phonograph turntable.

Other focusing objects can be used, but for the doctor's office the spiral will pay dividends in results obtained.

CHAPTER IV

THE MECHANICS OF HYPNOTIZING

A woman psychologist complained that she was afraid her voice was too high-pitched for her to be a good hypnotic technician. She felt that on occasion she was slow in hypnotizing a subject for this reason alone, and that consciousness of the deficiencies of her voice frequently made her lack confidence in the hypnotic situation. She believed that this feeling was communicated to the subject, and as a result her therapies were less effective than they might be.

The lady was right in thinking that her lack of confidence would be sensed by the patient, but her reason for feeling inferior was not justified by the facts. The chief agent in most hypnotic procedures is the voice of the hypnotist, but whether the voice is normally high-pitched or low-pitched is only a minor factor.

Of course, it is pleasant for an individual to have a good voice. But the important thing is to remember that the operator can move in a controlled fashion through the various phases that make up the hypnotic pattern by following a few simple voice techniques. These techniques can be used effectively regardless of the normal pitch of the voice. If the operator expresses confidence and self-assurance in speaking, he need not concern himself about the pitch of his voice.

Hypnotic trances, which are induced by "sleepy" or "relaxing" techniques, can be divided into three phases, considered from the standpoint of vocal technique.

1. THE LULLABY

In talking relaxation or sleep, the hypnotist is to a great extent duplicating the methods of a mother who sings a lullaby to her infant to induce slumber. The voice is deliberately made as soft and soothing as possible. Avoid harsh phrases. Use a tempo that is slow and monotonous. Croon or chant the words with a slight musical note, or simply speak in a soft murmur.

The voice need be no louder than to be heard distinctly by the subject. Even though the volume falls to very low levels, whispering is to be avoided. Whispering has a sibilant quality which tends to be stimulating rather than soothing. The timbre of the hypnotist's voice is probably most effective when used in a low murmur.

Avoid "stagey" and "dramatic" inflections and manners. Speak naturally and soothingly. Use your normal voice whether it is high-pitched or low.

Words should be chosen for their euphony. For example, "more heavy and more drowsy" are a trifle more soothing than "heavier and drowsier." The "ier" sound is slightly more harsh. "So-o-o sleepy" or "more and more sleepy" are better than "sleepier." A favorite phrase of many hypnotists is "deeper and deeper" or "deeper and deeper to sleep." These sounds are liquid provided the "p's" are slurred rather than exploded. A "Texas drawl" is excellent in the lullaby if not exaggerated.

2. THE SUGGESTION PERIOD

Suggestions may be given to the hypnotic subject in a normal, crisp, conversational tone. Speak as a salesman would to a prospect, confidently, firmly, authoritatively, with occasional emphasis when making a point clear. Talk at a vocabulary level where *every word* will be easily understood by the patient. Avoid speaking "up" or "down," don't be ingratiating or apologetic for what you are doing, and don't act "superior."

In making the transition from the lullaby phase to the suggestion phase, it is well to avoid sudden shock. Step the tempo up gradually. Increase the volume from a soft murmur to a conversational level in the course of several sentences, so that the subject is scarcely aware that a change has taken place.

It is worth noting that though the hypnotist should speak "authoritatively," this can be done in a "non-dominating" way. It is the quiet, self-confident expression of authority that is meant, not a bullying, dominating tone or manner. This might best be expressed with the thought: "We are going to do something together, but as I have more experience I will act as a guide" rather than "I am going to do something to you."

3. THE AWAKENING PERIOD

Be enthusiastic. Use superlatives. "Lay it on with a trowel." Do your best to imitate or even outdo our highly paid radio announcers who wax so enthusiastic over the merits of a miscellany of commercial products. Even though these radio annoucements may offend us because of their exaggeration, they do produce the identifications which lead us to buy these products in large quantities. "Sell" the subject the idea that when he awakens he is going to be refreshed and benefited by his hypnotic experience.

It is quite common—indeed, it is essential for the best type of awakening—to exaggerate beyond all the possibilities of "truth" in selling this idea to the patient. "Absolutely perfect," "rejuvenated," "better than you have ever felt before in your life"—the skilled hypnotist uses such extreme statements invariably, and so avoids the experience, occasionally encountered, of "refusal to awaken" on the part of the subject. (This problem is discussed at greater length in Chapter VI.) What seems to happen is that the idea of awakening is made so attractive to the subject that he is strongly motivated to awaken.

This is particularly important where the patient may have a neurotic compulsion to remain in the pleasant, relaxed world of hypnosis, and so escape from the burden of his waking troubles.

HYPNOTIC "PATTER"

A hypnotic "patter" may be likened to a brick wall. A smooth face of flowing suggestions is presented to the subject, but this face is actually composed of "bricks" of specific and motivating suggestions bonded together with a mortar of generalized "stock phrases" which tend to deepen the trance.

When puzzled as to the next step or procedure, the hypnotist covers his indecision by filling in with these stock phrases. As he utters them mechanically, he is considering the situation and selecting the next step in an unhurried manner. As soon as he has decided on a specific suggestion, he can make the transition from the stock phrase to the suggestion without the subject ever suspecting that there has been indecision.

This use of stock phrases explains the appearance of self-possession of the skilled hypnotist. He seems *always* to know what to say next, but only the untutored spectator is taken in.

The foregoing does not mean that an unbroken flow of conversation must always be kept up by the hypnotist. Before a period of silence, however, the subject should be given, either directly or indirectly, an understanding that when the hypnotist stops talking he does so deliberately rather than because he "doesn't know what to say next." For instance, the hypnotist might say, "Continue to relax more and more," or "Keep going deeper and deeper to sleep."

THE STRUCTURE OF AN
EDUCATION HYPNOSIS

During the initial period all suggestions tend toward impressing the patient with the following ideas which are also useful stock phrases. They are usually uttered repetitiously, and they should be drawn out. A list of them follows, with the drawn-out effect indicated.

"So-o-o-o sl-l-e-e-e-e-p-y-y, so-o-o-o sl-l-e-e-e-e-p-y-y, so-o-o-o sl-e-e-e-e-p-y-y."

"Mo-o-re and mo-o-o-re dr-ow-ow-ow-s-y-y, mo-o-o-re and mo-o-o-re dr-ow-ow-ow-s-y-y.'

"Mo-o-re and mo-o-re rel-a-a-xed, mo-o-ore and mo-o-ore rel-a-a-xed."

"Letti-i-ing go-o-oo."

"So-o-o-o comfortable."

"Loose"

"Limp"

"Heavy"

"Completely relaxed, every muscle relaxed."

The student hypnotist will find that with a little solitary practice in saying these words aloud in a soothing manner, he will soon be able to form the "habit" of speaking in this way with very little thought about what he is saying. Negative suggestions such as '"not uncomfortable" are taboo.

At some time in the lullaby, the hypnotist must arbitrarily assume that the patient is hypnotized. In eye fixation techniques, the moment of eye closure is assumed to be the point at which the patient "becomes hypnotized."

This is not necessarily so. A somnabulistic subject may be hypnotized for the first time while his eyes are still wide open. A patient with low suggestibility may close his eyes from fatigue and not be hypnotized at all.

As the student hypnotist gains experience, he will come to recognize many subtle indications of hypnosis. Some of these are hard to describe. Among the more obvious are complete physical relaxation, uncoordinated rolling of the eyeballs (with the eyes closed), a rapid vibration of the eyelashes, and the "sigh" or complete expiration of the breath, which is mentioned in many of the classical works on hypnosis. The hypnotic subject may exhibit none or all of these manifestations, but they form a guide which is generally useful.

After having observed "eye closure," or some other objective signs, which may indicate hypnosis, the operator will tell the subject plainly and directly that he *is* hypnotized, or "asleep" or "relaxed." He will then continue to deepen the trance with appropriate suggestions and stock phrases such as "You are going deeper and deeper to sleep," and "deeper and deeper, deeper and deeper, deeper and deeper." Such phrases are based on the idea that the subject is now hypnotized and is becoming more deeply hypnotized. Some operators prefer to equate the achieving of a deep response with the completion of some task such as hand levitation or the taking of ten deep breaths. These techniques are effective but not universally necessary.

Having told the subject that he is hypnotized, the next step is to tell him to "stay asleep" or "remain hypnotized" until you give specific suggestions for awakening. This can frequently be best done by giving a brief description of the advantages of remaining hypnotized and gaining the subject's consent. Suggest that he express his consent with a nod of the head.

If a more dominating method of hypnotic induction is used, the subject can simply be told to stay hypnotized until further notice, and to nod his head if he understands.

Such precautionary suggestions decrease the percentage of spontaneous awakenings. But even in spite of them, there will be an occasional awakening of this type. If the subject displays any uneasiness or anxiety symptoms when this suggestion is made, he can be told that you will awaken him instantly if he wishes you to, and that he can express his desire to awaken by a signal such as raising his left hand.

(Note: In such cases, do not make tests with the hand or arm which he is to use as a signal, and give him the specific suggestion that he can raise his hand easily at any time that he wishes to do so.)

The following outline gives a sharp picture of the step-by-step pattern that should be followed in the induction of an educational hypnosis:

1. You are becoming hypnotized.
2. You are hypnotized.
3. Your trance is deepening.
4. Stay asleep till I ask you to wake up.
5. Test for hypnotic response.
    (a) (optional) Describe test and gain subject's consent.
    (b) Make a detailed specific suggestion.
    (c) Challenge.
    (d) Withdraw the challenge.
    (e) Counter-suggest.
    (f) Test for normal reaction.
6. Suggestions for future response.
7. Post-hypnotic suggestions.
8. Amnesia suggestions.
9. Awakening techniques.
10. Tests of post-hypnotic response.

CHAPTER V

THE SCIENCE OF HYPNOSIS

VARIATIONAL RESPONSE IS COMMON

Human personalities may be considered as snow-flakes, all alike and yet infinitely varying, no two exactly the same. Successful hypotherapy is based, not upon the sterotyped recital of a verbal pattern, but upon the understanding of the underlying principles which determine the composition of verbal patterns. In this chapter we will consider methods which, when properly applied, enable the hypnotherapist to modify any technique to fit the personality of the individual subject. An understanding of these principles also enables one to formulate readily and easily suggestions to fit any specific situation.

Modern hypnotic experimentation began in the early nineteen twenties. Under laboratory conditions some older beliefs were confirmed, some were disproved and others still remain to be tested. The general pattern of the light, medium, and deep trances were known long before 1920, but is was L. W. Davis and R. W. Husband[9] who established a scale of tests which is now frequently used as a standard. The scale is as follows:

HYPNOTIC SUSCEPTIBILITY SCORING SYSTEM
(Davis and Husband)

Depth	Score	Objective Symptoms
Insusceptible	0	
	(1	
	(2	Relaxation
Hypnoidal	(3	Fluttering of lids
	(4	Closing of eyes
	(5	Complete physical relaxation
	(6	Catalepsy of eyes
Light Trance	(7	Limb catalepsies
	(10	Rigid catalepsy
	(11	Anaesthesia (glove)
	(13	Partial amnesia
	(15	Post-hypnotic anaesthesia
Medium Trance	(17	Personality changes
	(18	Simple post-hypnotic suggestions
	(20	Kinesthetic delusions and complete amnesia
	(21	Ability to open eyes without affecting trance
	(23	Bizarre post-hypnotic suggestions
	(25	Complete somnambulism
	(26	Positive visual hallucinations, post-hypnotic
Somnambulistic Trance	(27	Positive auditory hallucinations, post-hypnotic
	(28	Systematized post-hypnotic amnesias
	(29	Negative auditory hallucinations
	(30	Negative visual hallucinations; hyper-aesthesias

A more recent "yardstick" of hypnotic response has been compiled by LeCron and Bordeaux.[21]

SCORING SYSTEM FOR INDICATING DEPTH OF HYPNOSIS
(LeCron-Bordeaux)

Depth	Score	Symptoms and Phenomena Exhibited
Insusceptible	0	Subject fails to react in any way
Hypnoidal	1	Physical relaxation
	2	Drowsiness apparent
	3	Fluttering of eyelids
	4	Closing of eyes
	5	Mental relaxation, partial lethargy of mind
	6	Heaviness of limbs
Light Trance	7	Catalepsy of eyes
	8	Partial limb catalepsy
	9	Inhibition of small muscle groups
	10	Slower and deeper breathing, slower pulse
	11	Strong lassitude (disinclination to move, speak, think, or act)
	12	Twitching of mouth or jaw during induction
	13	Rapport between subject and operator
	14	Simple posthypnotic suggestions heeded
	15	Involuntary start of eye twitch on awakening

	16	Personality changes
	17	Feeling of heaviness throughout entire body
	18	Partial feeling of detachment
Medium Trance	19	Recognition of trance (difficult to describe but definitely felt)
	20	Complete muscular inhibition (kinesthetic delusions)
	21	Partial amnesia
	22	Glove anaesthesia
	23	Tactile illusions
	24	Gustatory illusions
	25	Olfactory illusions
	26	Hypercuity of atmospheric conditions
	27	Complete catalepsy of limbs or body
Somnambulistic or deep trance	28	Ability to open eyes without affecting trance
	29	Fixed stare when eyes are open; pupillary dilation
	30	Somnambulism
	31	Complete amnesia
	32	Systematized post-hypnotic amnesias
	33	Complete anaesthesia
	34	Post-hypnotic anaesthesia
	35	Bizarre post-hypnotic suggestions heeded
	36	Uncontrolled movements of eyeballs; eye coordination lost

37 Sensation of lightness, floating, swinging, of being bloated or swollen, detached feeling

38 Rigidity and lag in muscular movements and reactions

39 Fading and increase in cycles of the sound of operator's voice (like radio station fading in and out)

40 Control of organic body functions (heart beat, blood pressure, digestion, etc.)

41 Recall of lost memories (hypermnesia

42 Age regression.

43 Positive visual hallucinations; post-hypnotic

44 Negative visual hallucinations; post-hypnotic

45 Positive auditory hallucinations; post-hypnotic

46 Negative auditory hallucinations; post-hypnotic

47 Stimulation of dreams (in trance or post-hypnotic in natural sleep)

48 Hyperaesthesias

49 Color sensations experienced

Plenary Trance   50 Stuporous condition in which all spontaneous activity is inhibited.
Somnambulism can be developed by suggestion to that effect.

This scale is much more complete and useful as a working tool, but it also presents problems which can be solved only by mass experiment. Response No. 13, "Rapport between subject and operator," may be considered an open question. Hull[15] considers "rapport" to be a suggested phenomenon. It has been proved to exist without specific conditioning.

Number 22, "Glove anaesthesia," has been properly placed in the medium rather than light trance classification, but the label "glove anaesthesia" is in itself a misnomer. It is taken from descriptive psychiatry and is defined in Hinsie and Shatzky's "Psychiatric Dictionary" as "a disorder in the sensory field in which the patient has no sense of feeling in the area roughly corresponding to that covered by a glove; this anaesthesia is believed to be psychogenic."

"No sense of feeling," a complete anaesthesia, is listed as No. 33, a deep trance response. Number 22 should then be "localized analgesias" or insensitivity to pain with a full response to pressure or other stimuli. It can be induced in other parts of the body as easily as in the hand or arm.

COMPARISON WITH INDUCTION
TECHNIQUE OF CHAPTER II

It will now be seen that the induction technique of Chapter II utilizes a series of light trance tests which are progressively more difficult, then jumps to a medium trance test (the post-hypnotic handclasp) and ends with amnesia, which is now recognized as a deep trance test. The technique, accordingly, provides a check on the depth of trance attainable by the subject. As has already been stated, it will usually be found that one out of five will attain amnesia the first time. These can immediately be conditioned for an instantaneous response with the reasonable assurance that they will thereafter respond in a few seconds if the proper pattern of induction has been followed. A slightly larger percentage will have a partial amnesia and/or the post-hypnotic handclasp. But the majority who respond at all will achieve one or more of the light trance tests and will fail completely the first time in the medium or deep trance reactions. All of these can be conditioned to swifter response in each successive induction. Such are the facts based on an immense total of separate inductions made by leading scientific workers in the field.

RESPONSES NOT ALWAYS TO
PATTERN

There are people who will respond to a "light hand" before they will "take" an eye catalepsy. Others obtain the heavy or rigid arm first. There are individual variations. Operators and subject should be alert for such deviations and should never assume that the failure to achieve any particular test is a proof that the induction itself is a failure.

REASONS FOR VARIATIONS IN
RESPONSE

The eye catalepsy, rigid arm and heavy arm tests are all inhibitory responses. The subject is told that he *cannot* open his eyes or lift his arm or bend his arm. There are people who resist being restricted, and who object to being told that they will not be able to do something. This applies even where they have agreed to cooperate in the tests because frequently the resistance is on the unconscious and not the conscious level. In many cases the subject feels that he is surrendering his ego to the control of another person if he yields to an inhibitory test. For people like this, the light arm is often a way to success. It is positive, not negative. The subject's role is to remain passive, and "pay no particular attention to your arm and it will come up of its own accord." The fact that these variations exist does not mean that the operator should avoid the "catalepsy" tests. On the

51

average, they are achieved more swiftly than the "light" arm, which sometimes requires as much as thirty minutes for the first time.

WHAT IS HYPNOSIS?

Hypnosis has many times been likened to normal slumber and perhaps the most famous exponent of this definition is Professor Ivan P. Pavlov.[28] He says:

"We have established beyond doubt that sleep is inhibition spreading over all the hemispheres (of the brain). We have also been able to study the intermediate phases between the waking state and complete sleep—the hypnotic phases. These phases appear to us as ... different degrees of the extent of the inhibition in the areas of the hemispheres themselves and also in different parts of the brain; and ... as different degrees of intensity of inhibition at one and the same place. Naturally, with the greater complexity of the human brain, the hypnotic phenomena are considerably more varied in the human than in the animal. But it is possible that some of the hypnotic phenoma ... are more clearly marked in the animal, the more so because human hypnosis presents considerable variations depending upon the individual and the methods of hypnotization."

If we accept Pavlov's definition of hypnosis we might consider the "waking state" as white, and the slumber of exhaustion as black. Hypnosis, then, would correspond to the shades of gray which lie in between black and white. The rigid, inflexible person who maintains his character defenses to the point of unconsciousness recognizes only black and white.

The authors could have wished that Pavlov had discussed the state of deep trance wherein the subject is brought to the alert, eyes open, apparently normal in every respect, able to participate intelligently in the conversation, and yet throughout responds instantly to any test, including visual

52

and other hallucinations. In other words, the subject is obviously in the deepest possible trance state, yet able to think, reason, *work,* and in every way appear to use all his faculties. It is very difficult to accept the theory that a person in such a state is partially asleep. It is possible that Pavlov has part of the answer, and then again it is possible that he is completely wrong. Where hypnosis is concerned, the most eminent medical and scientific authorities have made statements which, to say the least, have been incautiously worded. Karl A. Menninger[25] lists fifteen types of psychotherapy broken into two divisions, one using the principle of suppression, the other the principle of expression. In the former he lists hypnosis, in the latter hypnoanalysis. For instance, he puts hypnosis in the same category as exhortation, persuasion and command, and hypnoanalysis with psychiatric counsel and psychoanalysis.

But hypnosis *of itself* is a tool and not a therapy. The exhortation and command of the "classical" hypnotist was effective because the subject was in a state of hypnosis. The hypnosis sharpened the response to therapy. Similarly, hypnosis is used to facilitate psychoanalysis. An excellent example of the use of hypnosis in an otherwise typical Freudian psychoanalysis is recounted by Robert Lindner.[23] It is clear that Menninger failed to discriminate between hypnosis as a therapy, which it is not, and hypnosis as a method of implementing any therapy which is to be admistrated verbally. These are subtle differentiations, but one cannot accept as final a theory of hypnosis which does not take into account every observable and recognized phenomenon.

One theory of hypnosis is that it is a condition where the "conscious" and "unconscious" have been separated or disassociated. This continues to be plausible, mainly because one of the preliminaries to the trance is to tire and distract the attention of the individual with a spiral or other means of focusing his senses within narrow limits. And yet, to believe this hypothesis means that such a division of the mind must be accepted along with it.

We must always bear in mind that scientific exploration involves the use of "constructs," formulations of "as if." We observe a series of events which seem to have some correlation. We say that these events happen "as if" such and such were true. For the limited purposes of further investigation we will say that such and such is true. We have then developed a construct which is useful in our search for knowledge. In our research we will act as though our construct were real, but we always bear in mind the fact that our construct is a theory or a fiction, a useful device but not necessarily true. The "conscious" and "unconscious" minds are constructs. They do not exist separately in reality.

Present day knowledge of hypnosis might be roughly compared to the knowledge of electricity half a century ago. The electron was unknown and so it was impossible to define electricity as a flow of electrons through a conducting material. And yet, though no definition was possible, a mighty science and a mighty industry were growing and new uses for electricity were discovered daily. It might be said, therefore, that some as yet undiscovered psychological or physiological or psycho-physiological "electron" may give us, in time, a theory of hypnosis which will account for all the observed phenomena. At present, we must be content to say that we do not know *what it is*, but we are beginning to understand how it works.

HOW THE THERAPY WORKS

According to Alfred Korzybski,[18] our emotions seem to be the product of the predominantly thalamic regions of the brain, in which lie the reactions of identification and of the automatic responses of the mind. The function of discrim-

54

ination seems to be restricted to the predominantly cortical areas. All psychotherapy is directed toward integrating the emotional and intellectual reactions of the individual to reality. In the various "schools" of psychology we find varying explanations for the cause and structure of psychological malfunction. The one point on which all the schools seem to agree is that the patient must obtain an emotional (that is, thalamic) reaction before permanent beneficial change can be achieved. Patterns of reaction must be altered. Hypnosis offers us a method of inhibiting the critical cortical activity while the desired emotional reaction is skillfully evoked. On its highest level, the knowledge of the operator cannot be too great. A comprehensive understanding of medicine, psychology and psychoanalysis is necessary if the permanent "cure" of some patients is to be achieved. Fortunately, many patients have *comparatively* minor problems. Often, in such cases, mere affirmations of health and well-being will produce excellent reactions. It is important, however, that the wording of all therapies, of whatever degree, follow the patterns now recognized as essential for the best results.

STRUCTURING THERAPEUTIC SUGGESTION

In using "waking suggestion" or heterohypnosis—hypnosis under the guidance of an operator—formulate your suggestions as follows:

1. *Use the present tense.* State it as an accomplished fact. In many cases, of course, a progressive development must be suggested. It is obviously nonsense to tell an ill patient, "You are well." But a change can be initiated by the suggestion, "You are becoming well" rather than the more indefinite, "You will become well." Even specific suggestions for future behavior can be given in the present tense, for example, "Next Thursday you are able to do this."

55

Right: "You are ... You feel ... Your (organ) is ... This is the way it *is*..."
Right: "You are becoming ... Your (condition) is changing..."
Wrong: "You will ... You will feel ... You will be..."

2. *Be positive.* Eliminate every possible negative word. That is why it is important to *read* the therapies given elsewhere in this book until positive statements have become habitual. Practically every emotional or physical condition can be expressed in a positive manner. Use the positive antonym. For example, in working with phobias, if we say, "You are not afraid" we are creating a large picture of FEAR with a small label "not this." Our patient will frequently see the picture without noticing the label, and react to the picture.
Right: "You are poised, you are self-confident, you are courageous, you are friendly."
Wrong: "You are not afraid, you are not self-conscious, you are not shy, you do not have stage fright."

3. *Be specific.* Analyze the psychological and physiological needs of the patient. Break the syndrome down into specific symptoms and, if possible, break the symptom down into specific reactions. Formulate a separate suggestion for each reaction.
Right: "This muscle (touching) is now relaxing, letting go. It is loose and limp, flexible."
Wrong: "You don't have backache any more."

4. *Be detailed.* Elaborate the suggestion until it covers the patient's possible reaction quite completely.

CHAPTER VI

TECHNICAL QUESTIONS

VARIATION IN SPEED OF RESPONSE

Some people can attain "deep" somnambulism in a matter of seconds. Others may require many hours of training before achieving the "light" trance. A number of busy physicians known to the authors have found it expedient to have an assistant do the conditioning of their less responsive patients. Such an assistant, nurse, hypnotic technician, etc., teaches the patient over a period of time to achieve hypnosis rapidly, whereupon the physician takes over and administers the therapy.

CONDITIONING
FOR INSTANTANEOUS RESPONSE

The exact wording for such conditioning is given in paragraphs 39 and 40 of Chapter II. Paragraph 39 is in a "high" vocabulary for more sophisticated and possibly more rigid subjects. Paragraph 40 is a simply worded version of the same thing.

It is important to understand and recognize the various kinds of response, how the slow subject can be conditioned to fast response, and how the fast subject can be conditioned to instantaneous hypnosis.

AWAKENING PROCESSES

The rule on awakenings is, if the induction has been slow

the awakening should be slow, if the induction has been fast awakening can be equally swift.

The slow awakening should follow the wording at the end of the long induction technique of Chapter II. The fast awakening has many variations but the following pattern is effective. It is briskly spoken:

"At the count of *three* you'll be *wide awake,* full of *pep* and *energy,* feeling *alert* and *cheerful. Wake up*—one—two—three!"

WHAT TO SAY WHEN HYPNOSIS IS ACHIEVED WITHOUT PER-MISSION

The operator should make a point of asking for permission to hypnotize. But sometimes he will forget, and in such an event, if the subject also forgets, he may have the experience of having achieved hypnosis without consent (apparently) having been given.

There are several reasons for this. The subject has come to the operator for the express purpose of being hypnotized. He has lost his early fears of hypnosis, and he is now aware that he can reject unwanted suggestions. He has confidence in the integrity of the operator, and he *knows* that the opertor is merely a guide to help him hypnotize himself. Under these conditions, hypnosis is sometimes attained without verbal consent, though the *conscious* willingness of the subject to be hypnotized is still the dominating factor.

CAN AN UNSCRUPULOUS PERSON MAKE USE OF HYPNOSIS?

It is probable that among the readers of this book will be a few whose eyes, as the saying goes, will "narrow with calculation" at the possibilities of hypnosis as a means of controlling other people.

"Suppose," they will say, "that I omit the conditioning

whereby I have to secure the subject's permission, but simply say to him, 'From now on, it will be possible for you to be hypnotized easily and swiftly when I snap my fingers and say, "Sleep." When I do that you will immediately go into a deep trance, and will thereafter do exactly as I say.' "

That, as will be seen, is a straightforward presentation of the problem. The theory, however, unfortunately for those who hold it (and fortunately for the rest of us) is based upon false folk beliefs about hypnosis. In order to make a personal use of hypnosis, it is first necessary to trick the "conscious" mind of the subject. Logical reasoning, persuasive double talk, advertisements, salesmen, and other glib means are some of the tools that do convince a normal person to follow a new course of action. But, having gone so far, hypnosis is no longer necessary. The victim is "convinced." Hypnosis can gradually change the direction of an individual's emotional reactions to life, but the conscious mind must participate in any quick, radical alteration.

THE HANGOVER

The "hangover" is a languorous condition. It is a result of an incomplete awakening, and usually occurs during the early stages of the training of a subject. The patient appears to be partially asleep or "dopey." Sometimes, there is an accompanying headache. The solution is to repeat the awakening suggestions with greater vigor, energy and enthusiasm. If the patient still remains in hypnosis, blow on his eyes and repeat loudly, "WAKE UP! WAKE UP! WIDE AWAKE NOW!" Do this several times if necessary.

Though harmless, the hangover should be watched for in the first few hypnoses of any patient. If not attended to, it may cause misgivings in the mind of a timid person.

RELAPSE INTO HYPNOSIS

Another minor problem of the hypnotist is the patient

who *refuses* to awaken from the hypnotic state, or, who having been awakened, relapses into hypnosis.

The easiest solution is to repeat the awakening suggestions forcibly as often as necessary. Sometimes, however, it is worthwhile to explore the condition thoroughly. There are two principal causes.

1. People who have been tensed for years find the relaxation produced by the hypnotic technique of Chapter II so satisfying that they do not want to come immediately back into the world of tension. For their benefit, insert some variation of the following words into the awakening technique:

"It is so very pleasant to be relaxed, so satisfying and restful. From now on, you are going to find it easier to relax whether you are in hypnosis or wide awake. It will be a progressive relaxation until finally your whole body is always in a state of dynamic relaxation, the relaxation of a champion athlete at the peak of his form. That's something to look forward to, isn't it? But now it's time to wake up."

Proceed with enthusiastic awakening technique of paragraph 46 of Chapter II.

2. Hypnosis can be an "escape" from reality. A person with a problem which seems unsolvable will sometimes sink into a "deep" somnambulism and try to remain there. This condition is frequently identifiable by the extreme laxness of the body, a state of limp relaxation.

If the patient is to be given therapy, the trance state now achieved can be utilized to probe for the problem that has caused it. Some of the questions the operator might ask are, "What is troubling you?" "What is on your mind?" "What are you thinking about?" "Is there any reason why you don't wish to wake up?"

Proceed with analysis if trained to do so.

It is possible to have curious experiences with subjects who have "escaped" into somnambulism. One patient not only relapsed into a "deep" trance but into an automatic age regression. The problem that was bothering her had apparently had its origin when she was two years old, and it was to the age of two that she reverted. She began immediately to cry as a baby cries.

The situation was further complicated by the fact that the psychologist knew her by a name which had never been used when she was a child.

The only danger in such an occurrence is that the unnecessary alarm of the amateur hypnotist may frighten the patient. An experienced hypnotic operator is *never* excited. No matter what happens he is curious and patient. He explores the situation, and does what is necessary.

In the instance mentioned, the psychologist quickly suspected the age regression and brought the subject back to the present.

HYPNOTIC TECHNIQUES NOT ALL VERBAL

The amount of suggestion necessary to obtain any single response varies with the intelligence, depth of trance and amount of training of the subject. All that is really necessary is that the subject "get the idea." For instance, with a trained subject the eye catalepsy suggestion can be condensed to "now your eyes are locked tightly closed, try to open them, but you can't." A rigid arm catalepsy can be induced by lifting the arm of the trained subject, extending it, folding the fingers into a fist and giving a light, vigorous grasp to the muscles of the fore and upper arm. The subject will understand and the catalepsy will be as effective as though you had spoken a hundred words.

The stage hypnotist uses a technique which is a far cry from "May I please hypnotize you?", "Yes," and "Sleep now!" He simply tells the subject, who is in a medium or

61

deep trance, about as follows: "After you wake up I will point my finger at you. Your eyes will instantly focus on the tip of my finger. Then they will close. You will instantly go to sleep, instantly. I may do it immediately, it may be an hour, it may be a year, but the next time I point my finger at you, you will instantly go to sleep." Such a technique works on naive subjects.

Or, again, the hypnotist may say, "The next time I take off my glasses you will become very sleepy and go right to sleep just as you are asleep now." Or perhaps, "Every time you sit down in the red chair you get so sleepy that you can't stay awake. You go right to sleep just as you are now."

Such suggestions have nothing to do with permission and apparently the hypnotist is riding rough-shod over the subject's desires. Actually, such is not the case. If the subject has any real objection to responding, he will not be hypnotized. The idea of permission is not to safeguard the subject but actually to safeguard the hypnotist from the misconceptions of the subject. It is highly advisable in the therapeutic situation.

On the other hand, in hypnoanalysis it is sometimes advisable for the therapist to appear to retain complete control of the situation. In such cases the permission technique would not be used. Any signal that is understood by the subject can be used to induce hypnosis once the subject has gone deep enough to achieve post-hypnotic responses. The signal can be auditory, a sentence, a word or a sound; for instance, a bell. It can be visual, a gesture on the part of the operator or some mechanical motion. It can be tactile, a touch in a certain manner. Although the authors are not aware of experiments with olfactory or gustatory stimuli, they believe that these senses too could be used to induce a hypnotic response where the subject is properly conditioned.

In the use of the "Consent, Sleep now!" technique you may occasionally encounter an aversion to the use of the word "Sleep." You will frequently encounter such idiosyn-crasies. They are nearly always due to an identification. In such cases merely substitute the word "Relax" for the word "Sleep."

Any verbal formulation can be used, but in working with large numbers of patients it is highly advisable to standardize on one or two verbal signals.

THE GOOD SUBJECT

Subjects who respond swiftly are of the class known as the somnambulists. They belong to the 20%, plus or minus, group who are easily hypnotizable by almost any method. In a doctor's office they will stare at the spiral for a short time, then their eyes will begin to water or flicker, and close. The alert operator will immediately skip to paragraph 16 of the induction and proceed from there.

If it is a first induction, he will be wise to take the tests one by one, but if he has proved at least once to the subject and to himself that the tests are all effective, then a quicker method is in order. Give the "eyes closed tight," or the "rigid arm" test, and from there jump to automatic motion. If response is swift in both cases, then the subject is probably ready to be conditioned for instantaneous hypnosis.

IMPORTANCE OF ESTABLISHING TRUST

It has been the concern of the authors to provide a detailed ethical approach to hypnosis in this volume. However, readers seeking a refutation of all the nonsense or a reaffirmation of what is now scientifically established or hypothesized about hypnosis should turn to one or more of the many *general* books on the subject. This work is designed to give word-for-word techniques for some of the more common therapeutic uses to which hypnosis has been and can be applied, and there are related chapters which are intended to explain and clarify the techniques.

Erickson[10] states that hypnosis cannot be used for criminal or antisocial purposes. But an ethical approach is essential in order to gain the confidence of the vast public whose knowledge of hypnosis consists of a number of fearful legends. Every doctor and operator who uses ethical methods will find it more and more easy to use hypnosis in his practice. On the other hand, the operator who fails to reassure his subjects will create mistrust and will thereby strengthen the fears of the people in his neighborhood. He will have gained nothing.

CHAPTER VII

DISGUISED HYPNOSIS—
ITS USE IN THERAPY

Miss J. came into Dr. N's office, and her condition was immediately brought to the doctor's attention by his nurse. The woman was trembling, her face was drawn into lines of fatigue; she appeared to be in a state of ultimate exhaustion. Normally, she would have been given a sleeping powder and told to go home to bed.

Dr. N. decided to use a disguised form of hypnosis. It seemed clear to him that this was no time to use an overt technique, since that would require explanations,, permission, and possibly there would be the added complication of the tension of fear.

He brought out his spiral. He explained casually that it was a device for inducing relaxation, and that it and similar relaxing methods were coming into wider use with medical men.

At no time during the induction technique that followed did he use the phrase, "going deeper and deeper," or "going fast asleep." Invariably, he employed instead the substitute phrase, "relaxing more and more ... " He did not hesitate, when the time came, to test for hypnotic response, and secured in quick succession eye closure, light arm, and automatic motion. In the end he wakened her with a vigorous suggestion for future well-being.

He reported a remarkable change in the woman. The lines of tension were gone from her face. She had stopped trembling. She left his office professing to feel more refreshed than she had ever been before in her life. Possibly for the first time since she had become an adult she was fully relaxed.

DISGUISED AID TO ANAESTHESIA

On another occasion, Dr. N. was acting as anaesthetist for a colleague for an operation. The patient began to moan and complain sleepily of pain. This went on for some time, and, though it seemed doubtful that there actually was pain in view of the amount of anaesthetic that had been administered, Dr. N. decided finally to use a disguised hypnotic technique on the restless patient. It was impossible, of course, to have a focusing object, so he began stroking the man's forehead, and talked relaxation. The groaning ceased. There were no further complaints of pain. The patient fell into a deep, relaxed sleep, and the operation continued without further incident.

DEFINITION

The two incidents described in the foregoing give a small picture of the possibilities of disguised hypnotic technique. Just in case there is any doubt, the dictionary meaning of "disguised" is applicable. In a disguised technique the patient does not know that he is hypnotized at the time of induction nor, when it is over, that he has been hypnotized.

THE ETHICS OF DISGUISED HYPNOSIS

At first thought it might appear that the disguised techniques are unethical. It might appear, too, that there is no reason why disguised hypnosis should ever be used. The logic behind such a negative approach goes something like this: Why bother with people who, for one reason or another, refuse hypnosis by name? Why not just tell them that the therapy is available, that it might benefit them, and let it go at that. It's their "funeral," not the doctor's.

As will probably be realized to some extent from the examples already given, such questions and attitudes reflect the doubts and anxieties of the newcomer in the field. Though the average doctor may not know it, the success of his "bedside manner" depends upon how closely he patterns the words he uses upon the verbal techniques described elsewhere in this book. By becoming aware of the principles underlying the methods which have been widely used for so many generations by medical men, the doctor will quickly discover how he can amplify his own vague methods by the more exact systems of hypnotic suggestion.

Many doctors, who may have felt on occasion that their over-effusive manner is resented by some patients, can now smooth off their false sounding "verbalisms" and substitute the tested positivities of hypnosis.

The disguised technique should not, of course, be used indiscriminately. This is not because it is dangerous, nor because it might be misused, but because the very necessity of keeping the patient from knowing that the technique is hypnotic limits its value. It is one of the tools which the good hypnotic technician employs as the individual need may arise.

HOW THE TECHNIQUE WORKS

The disguised technique consists of variations of the relaxation method given in detail in Chapter II, but without any reference to hypnosis or to sleep either before, during, or after the induction is administered. The problem, as with the other verbal techniques, is to become so familiar with the patterns that wrong words are simply not used. It need hardly be pointed out that one slip of the tongue would be a giveaway to some intelligent patients.

IF THE PATIENT SUSPECTS
THAT HYPNOSIS IS BEING USED

It will happen occasionally that a patient will become openly suspicious of the technique. This does not necessarily mean that he will object to the process, or even that he will resist. But there are several responses which the doctor can make in the event that the subject states his suspicion.

First of all, of course, under no circumstances should the physician become confused. He might say, "This is a form of relaxation that has been coming into wider medical use."

(That statement is true. Various methods of relaxation have been employed for years by doctors. All of these methods, without exception, can be carried on until a deeper hypnotic state is achieved.)

IN THE DISGUISED TECHNIQUE
TESTING FOR DEPTH

Many times it will be unnecessary to attempt the formal tests, which show what depth of trance has been attained. The desired response may be achieved without the necessity of asking for the rigid arm or for eye closure, let alone amnesia. In some cases, even the most arrant beginning hypnotist recognizes when he has gained his purposes. The skillful technician observes a dozen signals which the subject gives unconsciously. The LeCron-Bordeaux scoring table lists a number of these signals.

An example of the type of patient who does not have to be openly tested is the individual who is being given a physical examination but is so tense that the examination is being hindered. By using tactile stimulation and talking about relaxation, the physician can discover by probing when the desired response has been achieved.

However, the time will come when the deep trance is desired, and then the formal tests become necessary. The great majority of patients will accept the tests literally without surprise, argument, or objection. It is advisable, nevertheless, to offer some explanation.

One doctor on reaching the stage of testing for depth, always paused to say that this was a method of inducing relaxation, and that it had been discovered that, when the body is relaxed, the "unconscious" mind became highly susceptible to suggestion. This doctor calls the result "subconscious activation."

The physician who has reached the stage where he wishes to test for depth might well pause before trying for eye closure, and say in a casual tone:

"You know, you've now reached a stage of relaxation where some very interesting things can be done with your muscles. Just continue to lie (or sit) relaxed while I tell you a little bit about it. I don't know whether you've ever tried it or not, but if you stand in a doorway and press with your hands as hard as you can against the sides of the doorway— you'll have to keep your arms straight while you do it— you'll find that when you step out of the doorway, and stop pushing, your arms have a tendency to lift up in the direction that you were pushing. What has happened—at least this is what we think has happened—is that your unconscious mind continues to activate the nerves leading to those muscles, and so the arms appear to come up automatically.

"The human body, when properly relaxed, can do a lot of things like that, and I want to try a couple of them on you for a reason that I'll explain presently. Now, just relax a little more. Relax completely. Your eyes are becoming very heavy." (Proceed with eye closing test as given in paragraph 20 of Chapter II.)

WHEN DISGUISED TECHNIQUES ARE USABLE

There is no absolute rule as to when a doctor should employ hypnosis by name and when he should use hypnosis without naming it in any way. However, the following suggestions will be helpful. A disguised technique might be used in the following instances:

1. On individuals who, in the doctor's opinion, would be afraid of hypnosis by name.

2. On people who might agree to be hypnotized but who, in the doctor's opinion, would resist trance either consciously or unconsciously at a time when quick results are desirable.

3. On patients who have come to the doctor's office in a state of hysteria.

4. On a person who is ill and under too great a strain to be subjected to the necessity of deciding about "open" hypnosis.

5. During a physical examination, where the patient is too tense to be properly examined.

6. During operations, on patients who complain that the drug anaesthesia, either "total" or local, is not adequate.

TACTILE STIMULATION

In the disguised technique, a tactile stimulation is frequently used. This is an important feature of the skillful and casual disguised method. A word-for-word technique is given in Chapter VIII.

Let us suppose that a patient has come into your office feeling tired or ill, and in your opinion hypnosis would be of value. Say to him, "I have a relaxing method that will fix you up if you will just lie down and let me rub your neck or head."

Actually, you can rub the neck or stroke the hair or just massage the base of the skull, or the temples, or move your fingers across the forehead. The touch should not be heavy.

The manipulation of the muscles is not what is wanted in this technique. What seems to be important is the sensation that is produced on the skin by a light, gentle, monotonous tactile stimulation.

Begin immediately to talk relaxation. Use phrases like, "Just relax, let all tension fade out, just relax a little more, let all your muscles go limp." It is possible to go along in this fashion without ever mentioning the word "sleep." After a while, say, "This will make you feel a lot better. This will help your headache (or whatever the problem is). You will notice it getting better right away."

Proceed with other therapeutic suggestions. At no time is it necessary to use a visual method of fascination. The stimulation by the fingers is sufficient.

OTHER METHODS OF
STIMULATION EQUALLY USEFUL

Tactile stimulation is but one method of disguised hypnosis. Auditory and visual techniques are by no means ruled out. Any good mechanical gadget on which the attention can be fixed is good, particularly one with a rhythmical sound. An electric fan has quite a soporific effect. Even an electric refrigerator is good, or an electric bulb, either lighted or unlighted. The head of a nail, or a shiny ring, are both suitable. The important thing is to fix the attention of the subject on any one thing.

Say to the patient, "Just lie back and let the sound of that fan soothe you." Or say, "Look into that spiral, and let your whole attention be drawn into it." Or again, "We want to take your mind away from all the worries you've had today, so just watch that nail, watch it while we relax every muscle in your body. Fix your attention on that nail so that none of your troubles and worries can interfere while we relax your body." And so on.

THE FORMULATION OF THERAPEUTIC
SUGGESTIONS FOR USE WITH
DISGUISED TECHNIQUES

Elsewhere in this book, in giving the rules for the formulation of suggestions, we have stated that these suggestions should be made in the present tense.

The rule does not apply where the subject is unaware that he is being hypnotized.

Suggestions given to the hypnotized subject for extreme relaxation and anaesthesia, and post-hypnotic suggestions (such as continued freedom from tension, freedom from emotional depression, and even post-hypnotic anaesthesia) can be stated in the present tense because they can be explained as by-products of "extreme relaxation."

For other suggestions the patient must be given a basis for accepting the idea. For this purpose the placebo is an excellent tool. The physician can casually but forcefully mention to the hypnotized subject the fact that he is giving the patient a specific medicine which will do a specific job. He can describe the effect on the patient in great detail. He can then administer the placebo while the subject is "relaxed," "so that the medicine will have the best opportunity to act."

Suggestions for future changes in the physical or emotional condition of the patient can also be based on therapy which has been in progress or upon a comtemplated therapy. In this case the suggestions must be formulated in the future tense. In all cases where a disguised technique is being used, avoid the type of suggestion which has no rationale.

Give the patient a reason for what you are doing.

CHAPTER VIII

TECHNIQUES OF DISGUISED HYPNOSIS

"RELAXING" THE PATIENT

Before using this technique, determine the patient's reaction to "being touched." Some individuals find the close personal touch involved in this technique disagreeable. For these few the effect of "back rubbing" is to increase the tensions rather than to relax them. The great majority, however, will find the method very soothing. For the few exceptions, use a disguised visual fixation technique, or one of the other methods described in the preceding pages. (A word-for-word technique for the eye method begins on page 12).

Place the patient face down on a couch, treatment table, bed, etc., in a comfortable, prone position. Make sure that earrings, belt buckles, things in the pockets, and other lumpy objects, will not interfere with the patient's comfort when he is fully relaxed. Use a gentle, soothing touch. This is not a massage to break the muscle tension by force. It is a friendly "caressing" type of touch, the kind you would use in petting a dog or cat, firm and gentle, not vigorous.

Now, close your eyes and let yourself become as limp as possible. Let your mind drift. Make no effort at all. I'm going to rub your back for a little while. Enjoy this. Just rest and enjoy yourself while I rub your back.

Start rubbing the back. Concentrate on the shoulders at first. Gentle, soothing strokes back and forth across the shoulders up onto the sides of the neck, and a rotary stroke between the shoulder blades. Speak softly in lullaby fashion.

73

Everybody likes to have his back rubbed. Everybody likes to have his back rubbed. Having the back rubbed is a very primitive pleasure. This is probably the first one you experienced when you were a baby. When you were just a baby your mother used to rub your back to quiet you and comfort you. You learned to like having your back rubbed very early in life. You've seen it done to babies, too. You've seen a crying baby picked up by its mother. Baby stops crying almost right away just because mother has touched it. Then when mother pats the baby a little and rubs its back, baby gives a sigh of contentment, stops crying and relaxes just the way you're relaxing, relaxing more and more, relaxing more and more, all the muscles in your back are relaxing the way a baby relaxes, getting loose and limp and comfortable, so comfortable, so very comfortable.

Everybody likes to have his back rubbed. It's not only humans that like it. Even animals like to have their backs rubbed. Dogs and cats like it. Horses like it. Most animals like it. Have you ever had a kitten jump up on your lap? You probably have had a kitten in your lap at some time, and almost instinctively you start to stroke it just like this.

Change the stroke to a soft, downward rubbing along the spine. To carry out the identification, rub only from the shoulders down to the waist, not back. Stroke as though you were smoothing the fur of a cat.

As you stroke the cat's back, you can feel it relax just as your muscles are relaxing. I can feel them relaxing now, letting go, letting go. You are becoming comfortable, very comfortable, just like the cat. As you rub the cat's back, you can feel it relaxing more and more. Soon it starts to purr. The eyes become drowsy and narrow to slits. Soon they close as the cat relaxes more and more. If you keep on stroking, the cat will soon go to sleep. As you keep on stroking, the cat relaxes more and more, more and more, just as you are relaxing more and more.

74

Or maybe you've had a puppy come to you and beg to be petted. If you invite him, he will jump into your lap, and as you start rubbing his back, he too will relax. He especially loves to have you rub the base of his skull, just like this.

Use a gentle circular stroke at the occipital, thumb on one side, forefinger on the other. Alternate this with a gentle stroking of the trapezius muscles, carrying the stroke well down onto the shoulder.

As you rub the puppy's neck and shoulders, he will relax. You can feel his muscles letting go under your hand just the way yours are relaxing. The more you rub the more he likes it. As you rub, and he relaxes more and more, his eyes will close, and if you keep on rubbing long enough, the puppy will go to sleep. Everybody likes to have his back rubbed. Everybody likes to have his back rubbed. Everybody relaxes when his back is rubbed, just the way you're relaxing. You're feeling so comfortable, so peaceful, so relaxed, just like the kitten, just like the baby, just like the dog, comfortable, relaxed and drowsy.

Change the next line to suit your local conditions. The wording is for a city physician going to a riding club.

Last Sunday I spent a little time at the stables. The stableman was grooming the horses. He would lead one out and then start working with the brush and currycomb. How those horses did love it. Even a horse loves to have his back rubbed. The horses stood perfectly still and contented while they were rubbed and rubbed and rubbed.

Work on the lower back, stroking outward from the spine with alternate strokes on either side, or with several strokes to one side and then to the other. Occasionally work back up to the shoulders, and then down the spine.

It's such a natural thing to relax when your back is rubbed. Those horses certainly enjoyed their grooming. A horse will stand and let you rub him until your arms are weary. A horse can take more rubbing than you can give him. He never wants you to stop. Everybody likes to have his back rubbed. Everybody relaxes when his back is rubbed, just the way you are relaxing. You are so comfortable now, so peaceful, so utterly relaxed. Every muscle in your body is relaxed, loose, limp and flexible. As your muscles relax they feel heavy. You're feeling heavy all over now, very heavy. Your arms feel heavy. Your legs feel heavy. You are so relaxed that to move would require an almost impossible effort. Your body is heavy. Your neck is heavy. Your head is heavy. Even your face feels heavy. You are so utterly relaxed, and you are going to keep right on relaxing for a while, relaxing more with every touch of my hand, relaxing more with every deep, easy breath that you take.

By this time the patient is ready for suggestions, or other hypnotherapy. If the physician wishes to test the response, the following disguised eye catalepsy suggestion may be used. If no tests are desired, the hypnotherapy can be followed with a disguised awakening suggestion.

EYE CATALEPSY TEST

You feel so heavy, so relaxed and so heavy. Even your eyelids feel heavy, They feel so very heavy. Your eyelids are so heavy that it would require too much effort even to open your eyes. Your eyelids are so heavy, so very heavy, so heavy that even if you tried to open them they would not open. Your eyelids are too heavy to open. They are so heavy that it is quite impossible to open them. You can try to see for yourself, but you are so relaxed and your eyelids are so heavy that it is quite impossible to open them. They won't open. They are too heavy.

Watch for the first sign of an effort to open the eyes, such as movement of the eyebrows, or any movement of the face. If the eyes open say: "I'm surprised. I thought you were so relaxed that your eyes wouldn't open. But it's all right. Just close them, and we'll relax you a little more." *Continue rubbing the back and repeating "more and more relaxed, more and more heavy" for two minutes, and then go directly to the therapeutic suggestions without any further attempted test. On the other hand, if the eyes do not open, as soon as an attempt to open them has been made unsuccessfully, continue.*

You see, they're just too heavy. Don't bother to try any more. Don't bother to try to open them. Just relax even more, and become more and more heavy. You are having a wonderful rest and relaxation.

Use the desired therapeutic technique.

AWAKENING

Now, you've had a nice rest. You are thoroughly relaxed and a lot of this relaxation is going to stay with you. The next time you relax this way you're going to find it much easier to let go. The mere touch of my hand on your back is going to remind you of this experience, and so you will find it much easier to relax the next time. It will be very much easier the next time. Soon, we will have you so used to the idea that you will be able to stay much more relaxed all the time.

I'm going to rub a little more briskly now to encourage the circulation, and as I rub you will notice the heaviness leaving, and a wonderful feeling of vitality coming into all your muscles. As I rub you are going to feel more alert, and by the time we finish, you are going to feel filled with energy and pep.

Start rubbing briskly with light quick motions and a little more pressure than before. Continue this until the patient opens his eyes and finish off with a couple of quick pats on the shoulder.

You feel the pep flowing into your muscles. You feel more

77

and more energy, more and more vitality. Your circulation is speeding up now. You are feeling more and more alert, more and more alert. More and more alert. You feel wonderful. You're all ready to get up now, all ready to get up.

DISGUISED VISUAL TECHNIQUE
(For People Who Have Binocular Vision)

In using disguised techniques of hypnosis it is always well to have some "logical" reason for the occurrence of the sensations that the subject will experience. The physician who is hypnotizing a layman can use short "logical" pseudo-scientific explanations which will satisfy the mind of the patient. The physician gives him an "excuse" to experience the phenomena which will follow. In hypnotizing a fellow practitioner or other patient with a knowledge of physiology and psychology the explanation must seem reasonable to the subjcet. The following simple disguised technique would not be applicable to the sophisticated patient. Any simple object is suitable as a fixation point for this technique, a nail head on the wall, an electric light, the reflection of a piece of metal, or varnished furniture. The word "reflection" is in parenthesis in the following, so that any on of the focusing points can be substituted for it.

Many of our ailments and discomforts come from muscular tension. When we have remained tense for a long time we acquire a habit of tension. I guess we'll have to teach you how to relax. Sit down in this chair and make yourself comfortable. Separate your hands and let them lie loosely on your lap or the arms of the chair. Make yourself as comfortable as possible. Try to feel heavy. Now look at the (reflection) which you see over here while I tell you how this works.

We have discovered that one of the quickest ways to relax the entire body is to relax the eyes. If you look steadily at something like this (reflection) for a little while you will

78

eventually get a double image. You will see two reflections, one with each eye. That is, you will if you keep looking at the (reflection) without really trying to see it. We might say, look at it steadily but without much interest. Keep your eyes looking in that direction, the way you might look at a blank wall without particularly seeing anything of interest. Look through it rather than at it. As you watch the (reflection) in this disinterested fashion, you will notice a general clouding and fogginess of your vision. You might say that your eyes are getting bored. After a while you will notice the first relaxation. That will be when you see double. That means that the fusion centers in your brain are relaxing and that will quickly be followed by relaxation of the eyes and eyelids. They will stop working. Your eyelids will close. This will happen soon after you see double. Then when your eyes are closed the rest of your body will quickly relax also. This happens quite naturally because the eyes are so closely connected to the brain. You might say that the eyes are an extension of the brain. When your eyes relax, your optic nerve relaxes, and very quickly after that the whole brain relaxes. You will actually notice this as a slowing down in the thinking. You get a kind of a dreamy feeling. Your brain is actually relaxed, and then, of course, the whole nervous system follows right along. When the brain is relaxed all the muscles of the body begin to relax. All the muscles let go. Arms and legs become loose and limp. Shoulder muscles become soft and flexible. Your breathing becomes deep, gentle and rhythmic. As the hands and feet become more and more relaxed, you may notice a slight, pleasant tingling sensation in the toes and fingers. Then as you become more comfortable, you almost forget you have a body. As the various parts of the body become completely and utterly relaxed, you lose the sense of feeling in them. When nothing interesting is happening the senses don't work very hard.

With some quickly responsive patients the eyes will be closed at this time, and therapeutic type suggestions can be administered. With others who respond more slowly the following suggestion can be used.

Now just keep watching the (reflection) until you see double and your eyes close. I'm going to be busy for a little while, so don't pay any attention to me when I come in or go out. Just keep watching the (reflection) until your eyes close, and then let this whole cycle of relaxation take place. If I come in when you're relaxed, pay no attention. Just keep on relaxing more and more. I'll tell you when you've had enough. Now, I've got to go to work for a little while.

Upon returning to the room, or again turning your attention to the patient, if the eyes are still open, say, "I have the feeling that you are trying to watch the (reflection) too closely. Don't work so hard at it. Look through it, not at it." Repeat the paragraph immediately preceding.

If the eyes are closed, as they will be in most cases, re-establish contact with the following words.

Just keep on relaxing. Don't pay any attention to me. Keep on relaxing more and more. I'll tell you when you've had enough.

Give the therapeutic suggestions.

AWAKENING SUGGESTIONS

Now that you are thoroughly and completely relaxed, we want to get some pep and energy into you, and still leave those muscles loose and flexible. First of all, start noticing the little sounds around you. Hear the things that are happening outside. *(Pause.)* Now, open your eyes and we'll do a little exercise. First, look up, way up . . . now, down . . . way down, now way to the right, now way to the left . . .

Now let's do some stretching exercises, like a cat. Extend your fingers way out . . . now clench your fists . . . now open

80

and close them several times ... move your hands with a circular motion a few times ... Now stretch your arms way out to your sides, and stretch ...Now clasp them back of your head and stretch.

Now stand up and stretch as tall as you can ... really stretch out ... How do you feel?

CHAPTER IX

AUTOHYPNOSIS—ITS PLACE IN THERAPY

A physician received an emergency call from a patient who was suffering from an acute attack of asthma. On his arrival at the patient's home, the doctor decided to use a slightly disguised hypnotic technique. The patient sank into a light hypnosis. The asthma paroxysms stopped.

On his next call, the doctor was drawn aside by the patient's wife, who expressed the fear that her husband was going out of his mind. "He keeps talking to himself, doctor. He's in there now, muttering away." On being questioned, the patient divulged the following information: He'd felt so good after the doctor's verbal therapy that it stayed in his mind. The next time that he felt tensions building up, and an asthma paroxysm coming on, he tried talking to himself, and the words that his wife would have heard had she listened more intently were: "Arm is relaxing, every muscle relaxing, relaxing more and more, more and more." There was a method to this madness, for the therapy worked just as well for the patient as it had for the doctor.

This case demonstrates the ease with which some people can learn autohypnosis, and also the value of hypnosis in therapy.

WHAT AUTOHYPNOSIS IS

Autohypnosis is the ability to hypnotize oneself as easily and, with some qualifications, as effectively as it is possible to be hypnotized by another person. Though there are methods for learning the art of autohypnosis without the aid of a hypnotist (for instance, it is believed the Yogi learn autohypnosis in their religio-philosophical system), these methods require prolonged training and involve ascetisms not popular with the Western mind. The modern hypnotic technician trains a subject to respond first of all to outside suggestions, then to suggestions given by his own mind.

THE PURPOSE OF AUTOHYPNOSIS

A patient who has been trained to autohypnosis can use his ability to reinforce the "supportive" therapy given by his doctor. The effect of the suggestions received in the doctor's office may last a few minutes, a few hours, a few days, or not at all. But whatever its duration, it will seldom in the early stages of the treatment suffice the patient until his next appointment. In the days when hypnotic operators used "supportive" therapy without other psychotherapeutic techniques, this varying effectiveness of their suggestions brought hypnosis into disrepute with the therapeutic professions. It was so much easier to depend on drugs, which could be prescribed to be taken "after each meal" or "whenever you feel the pain coming back." Lacking any comparable relieving agent, many physicians abandoned the use of hypnosis, or else used it so cautiously that it was virtually valueless.

The ability to give oneself at will the therapy prescribed by the hypnotist-doctor is the hypnotic equivalent of the drug prescription. If it can be used at all, it is superior to some drugs in that it seems to work by bringing the functions of the body to a normal state for a greater or lesser period. The glands, the organs, the muscles, nerves, and blood actually appear to coordinate to bring the body as a whole back to a state of health. As the treatment progresses, and if the symptom is not too deep-seated (the more complicated problems require insight therapy) the symptom will gradually fade away.

This may happen even if the problem goes "deep," but in such cases it is important that there be a parallel use of psychotherapy on a "depth" level, or else another symptom may replace the one that has been unlearned.

Many patients do not have access to depth psychotherapy and must be content with "supportive" therapy only, either as a temporary analgesic or as a periodic reinforcement of a definite curative suggestion. For them, particularly, but also for those who can have depth psychotherapy, autohypnosis, where it can be used, is a short cut to better health and greater happiness.

AUTOHYPNOSIS AS AN EXPLANATION FOR ALL HYPNOTIC PHENOMENA

Among the divergent points of view concerning the nature of hypnosis, the concept that the phenomena are all autohypnotic has gained wide acceptance. The patient is "helped" to attain autohypnosis every time he is hypnotized. He "agrees" to the suggestions of the hypnotist, and without his unconscious agreement the suggestions do not take effect. The old belief that no person can be hypnotized against his definitely opposed will is true for the simple reason that hypnosis occurs "inside" the hypnotized individual, and is not an external event.

This does not mean that a person cannot be hypnotized against his conscious and expressed determination. The technique of the stage hypnotic showman, operating as it often does against people who are completely ignorant of what hypnosis can or cannot do, sometimes seems to achieve hypnosis regardless of the expressed desire of the subject. The reasons for this can be found in the false fear of the "victim" that he *can* be hypnotized against his will. If this fear is in the back of his mind, then his verbal protests are meaningless. He has to all intents and purposes "agreed" to the idea that he can be hypnotized.

CONDITIONING FOR AUTOHYPNOSIS

Chapter X provides a word-for-word technique for conditioning a subject for autohypnosis. The general principle of this technique is as follows: The patient is hypnotized and depth achieved. The subject is then taught to respond in an automatic and instantaneous (or very rapid) response to a given signal. He is tested under hypnosis, given a post-hypnotic suggestion, and awakened in a minute or so. If the post-hypnotic response is effective, then the subject is again hypnotized and this time he is given the post-hypnotic suggestion that he will respond to the signal when self-administered. In a similar manner he is conditioned to awaken himself from hypnosis at will. Finally he is taught how to give himself post-hypnotic suggestions which may be as effective as those of the physician.

MECHANICS OF AUTO-SUGGESTION

In formulating suggestions for the patient to use in autohypnosis, the following rules apply:

1. *Write it.* Write the suggestion out in accordance with the laws of hetero-hypnotic therapy as given in Chapter III. Writing forces us to crystallize our ideas. It makes us analyze the problem that we are facing, and is an aid to clear thinking.

2. *Symbolize it.* Give it a key word or idea, a code word. By definition, then, the symbol represents the entire formulation, exactly as in a trans-oceanic cable code a nonsense word may represent a complex sentence or idea. Select a simple word, preferably (but not necessarily) one that carries out the implication of the entire suggestion. For example, a therapy typed out single space and occupying a page which is designed to help a patient overcome feelings of inferiority could be symbolized with the word, "Confidence."

3. *Edit it.* Read the written suggestion to insure that it complies with the basic laws. Revise it. Reconstruct it. Expand it. Condense it. Recopy the revised version and destroy the first draft.

4. *Read it aloud.* Before hypnotizing yourself, carefully read the entire suggestion to yourself aloud. When in the presence of others where reading might be embarrassing or impossible, the suggestion can be read silently but very carefully. Reading aloud is preferable because it compels the uttering of every word. In reading silently, we are accustomed to scanning and skipping. When a suggestion has been properly edited, every word is important.

5. *Hypnotize yourself.* Use the particular method that has been taught to you. Such a method is given in Chapter VI.

6. *Think the symbol.* Or whisper it to yourself. Make no effort to remember what the symbol means or to think of the original suggestion. You have given yourself the suggestion fully and forcefully as a pre-hypnotic suggestion. You have, so to speak, loaded the gun. When you think the symbol, you are merely pulling the trigger on a gun which is already loaded. An alternate method, which is described by Victor Dane,[8] is to roll the paper containing the suggestion and hold it in one hand or tape it to the hand. The presence of the paper, which has been previously read, serves as a trigger.

A THEORY OF SYMBOL AUTOHYPNOSIS

It is hypothesized that in the state of hypnosis the cortical activity of the brain is reduced. In the light and medium trances, hypnotic operators have noticed again and again that cortical activity seems to be accompanied by a lightening of the trance condition and an accompanying lack of response to suggestion.

By pre-suggesting the entire concept, it can be triggered in hypnosis with an absolute minimum of cortical activity and a much greater attendant response. It is true that many well-trained somnambulistic subjects have acquired the ability to select, formulate, and self-administer complex suggestions while in the trance state. The explanation would seem to be that these subjects are so deep that even a considerable lightening of their trance state leaves them still in a position to obtain an adequate response. On the other hand, were this same feat attempted by a light or medium trance subject, his trance would be so so lightened that by the time his formulation was completed he would usually be in the hypnoidal or even in the full waking state, and would not be able to respond to his own suggestion.

The apparent exceptions previously mentioned illustrate the possibilities of the very deep trance. They do not apply to the average subject. The symbol should be an integral part of autohypnotic therapy.

IMPORTANCE OF UNIFORM
VERBAL PATTERN

In teaching autohypnosis, the following point should be made clear to the subject. Autohypnosis is primarily the establishment of a system of conditioned responses. In such conditioning, a specific stimulus elicits a specific response. Words or phrases which are used as key words or symbols must be used in a uniform manner if they are to achieve success. Confusion regarding the key word will produce failures.

An interesting example of this occurred when a man was conditioned to respond to autohypnosis with the key words, "Sleep now!" After a few satisfactory practice sessions, he found himself unable to induce autohypnosis. As he put it, "I relax, think the words, and nothing happens."

At the next consultation, the psychologist searched for half an hour for possible new factors which might have brought about a psychological resistance to the self-induced trance. Failing, he asked the patient to attempt to hypnotize himself. The subject composed himself and said, "Now sleep!" That simple transposition of the two words proved to have disturbed the fine equilibrium which had been achieved, and so the patient failed to achieve hypnosis. The patient was asked to use the original key word, "Sleep now!" The response was immediate and satisfactory.

Such cue words might be compared to so many Yale keys, which have been carefully manufactured to fit Yale locks. Any key will slide into any lock, but it can be turned only in the one to which it is fitted. The back door key won't fit the front door, etc. "Now sleep" is not the same as "Sleep now."

It is the awareness of, and attendance to, such details that distinguishes the expert hypnotist from operators who merely depend on the law of averages for any success which they may achieve.

CHAPTER X

CONDITIONING IN AUTOHYPNOSIS

Train the subject in hypnotic response until there is a definite and demonstrable post-hypnotic effect, such as the handclasp catalepsy. Work with paragraphs 38 and 39, or paragraph 40, Chapter II, until the subject has learned to respond to an instantaneous signal. Work with instantaneous responses until the subject can respond instantly with an interval of not less than 24 hours since the previous hypnosis. Hypnotize the subject, and proceed.

1. You are going deeper and deeper, deeper and deeper, deeper than ever before. Take a deep breath and as you exhale feel yourself going down, down, down, down, down deeper than ever before, deeper than ever before, deeper than ever before. Your right *(or left)* hand is going to feel light, and will float up into the air. It is beginning to feel light and soon it will float up into the air. It is beginning to feel light, and soon it will float up into the air. Your hand is getting lighter and lighter, lighter and lighter. Your hand is floating, floating, floating, up, up, up, up, up, up, up, up, up, up.

Continue repeating these last two sentences over and over until the hand has levitated two or three inches.

2. Now, the thumb and fingers are beginning to straighten out. They are straightening out. Your fingers are getting straighter and straighter. Your fingers are becoming so straight that they are curving backwards.

3. All the extensor muscles in your hand and forearm

are tightening up, tighter and tighter, tighter and tighter. Your hand is becoming stiff and rigid, stiff and rigid.

Continue repeating the last paragraph until the hand is rigidly extended.

4. Now, your hand is rigidly extended. It is impossible for you to clench your fist. It is impossible for you to clench your fist. Try to clench it, and you will see that you cannot do so. Your hand is rigid.

Wait for the subject to test it. Not much suggestion is required because of the level of hypnosis previously attained by the subject.

5. You see, your hand is completely controlled by your unconscious mind. Your hand is still rigid. Now, stop trying to clench it. It is still rigid. We are going to call this position "A." As you may know, the army used to symbolize a very complicated operation with a simple symbol. Operation "X" might mean a great deal. "X" might be the symbol for a complicated series of operations. In the same way "A" is the symbol for this position of your hand. "A" means that your hand comes to this position, with the fingers rigidly extended. "A" means that you cannot clench your fist. When I say "A," your unconscious mind will accept that sound as a signal to work all the muscles that brought your hand to this position. When I say "A," your hand will auomatically and rapidly come to this position. "A" is the symbol for this position of your hand.

6. Now we will have to have another symbol to represent the normal relaxed condition of your hand. For that we will use the letter "B." When I next say the second letter of the alphabet, the muscles in your hand and arm will relax instantly, and your hand will be normally responsive to your will. When I say "A," your hand comes to this rigid position. *(Give the order for subject's hand to relax, as follows:)* "B"—your hand is relaxed and normal.

As soon as the subject's hand has relaxed, continue.

7. "A."

Wait for the hand to come up to rigid position. In a well-conditioned deep trance subject, the response will be immediate. With some subjects, who have barely reached the level of post-hypnotic response, it will be much slower. In such slow cases, use the following:

8. "A." Your hand is coming up. "A." Your fingers are extending. "A." Your fingers and hand are becoming rigid. "A" ... "A" ... "A" ..."A"

Repeat these phrases over and over, building up the association with the sound of "A."

9. "B." You see your hand is now relaxed and normal. Your hand is responding to these symbols. **Again.** "A."

With a responsive subject you have already built up a conditioned response. When the response is slower, continue the technique of Paragraph 8 of this Chapter, over and over. As the response becomes faster, eliminate the suggestions and simply repeat "A," "A," "A" over and over again.

When the subject has achieved the point of conditioning at which he responds to your utterance of the word "A," without repetition, and without supporting suggestions, you are ready for the next step.

10. "A" ... "B" ... "A" ... Your hand is quite rigid, and it is impossible for you to clench your fist. Try to clench it. You see, it will not clench. "B." Now, I am going to show you an interesting thing. First of all, let me remind you that this is simply a signal. It is like a signal that you give a motorman when you want to get off the streetcar. You ring the bell. He stops the streetcar. There are lots of push buttons on the streetcar, and the motorman doesn't care whose finger pushes the button, nor which button is pushed. They all ring the bell. In the same way your un-

91

conscious mind does not care who gives the signals to your hand. Soon, I am going to ask you to say the first letter of the alphabet. It may surprise you when your hand acts exactly as it did when I said it. You can speak freely and easily; and go deeper to sleep as you speak. Now, please say the first letter of the alphabet aloud.

When the subject says "A," the hand will almost invariably respond. In some cases, it may be necessary for the operator to add a few supportive suggestions, "coming up, coming up," etc., but in most cases the response will be about the same as the last, previous response to the operator.

11. You see, your hand responds to the symbol when you give it exactly as it does when I give it. If you try to clench your fist, you will find that your hand is as rigid as before. You are the one who has made it rigid. Now, say the second letter of the alphabet... *(Patient does and the hand relaxes).* You see, your hand relaxes. "A" ...This time I gave the signal to make it rigid, but you give the other one. *(Patient says "B" and hand relaxes).* ... Now, say the first letter again... *(Patient says "A" and hand extends).* "B" —You see, it doesn't matter how we mix them up.

Practice this for a little while. If someone else is in the room, ask him to give one or the other of the signals a few times so that the subject can become thoroughly acquainted with the idea of a conditioned response.

12. Now, we have another surprise for you. Think the sound of the first letter. Say it to yourself. *(hand responds)* You see, your hand is responding to your thought. Your unconscious mind is taking orders from your conscious mind, and these orders must be obeyed. You'll notice that you cannot clench your fist now either ... Now, think the second letter and go deeper and deeper, deeper and deeper. After you awaken your hand will still respond to these sig-

nals for the *next five minutes*. Even when you are wide awake your hand will become completely rigid and fully extended if you think the first letter of the alphabet or if either of us says it. It will relax when you think or say, or hear the second letter of the alphabet. At the end of five minutes your hand will no longer respond to these symbols. They will have served their purpose.

Awaken the subject with the usual technique. Amnesia may be induced if possible. Wait after each letter in the following:

13. "A" ... "B" ... "A" ... "B." Interesting, isn't it? Try it yourself. Say the first and second letters of the alphabet and see what happens. Now, think them.

Experiment with the post-hypnotic response for a while, pointing out to the subject that after he has induced a catalepsy by saying or thinking the symbol that he is placed in the peculiar situation of not being able to clench his fist, and yet being able to clench it. That is, he cannot clench his fist without first giving himself the releasing signal, but he is free to give himself the signal at any time he wishes.

Rehypnotize the subject with your instantaneous technique. If you have followed the technique of Chapter II, paragraphs 39 and 40, the cue will be, "Sleep, now."

14. Deeper and deeper, deeper and deeper. Now, we are going to wipe out the responses to the letters of the alphabet. They are no longer necessary, so your hand no longer responds. "A" is just the first letter of the alphabet, and "B" is just the second. Your hand no longer responds. The letters mean nothing to you now. "A," "B," "A," "B." You see, your hand no longer responds.

15. You were taught this discipline so that you would have the knowledge which is given to us by experience. You have experienced the fact that you too may give the symbols which will produce a response in you. The words that I

used as a symbol for your present condition of hypnotic trance were "Sleep, now." It was necessary for you to give me permission before they would work. When you gave your permission they worked automatically. The words that I have been using to awaken you are, "Wake up!", followed by a count of three. If, when you are awake, you decide that you wish to be hypnotized, that is equivalent to giving me your permission. If you have decided that you wish to be hypnotized, all that you have to do in order to bring about a deep hypnosis is to say or think, "Sleep, now." At the word "now" you will become deeply hypnotized. With the word "now" you will relax and go into a very deep hypnosis. When you wish to awaken yourself, think or say the words "wake up" and then count to three. Those words mean to you, "I awaken refreshed. I awaken serene. I awaken intellectually alert, keen. I awaken emotionally calm and poised. I awaken vibrant with life and energy and vigor. I awaken refreshed and rested. I awaken physically perfect, mentally perfect, emotionally perfect." The simple words, "Wake up—one, two, three" are symbols which automatically induce these conditions of awakening. Now, awaken yourself by saying, "wake up—" and counting to three. Wake yourself up. You can do it.

If the patient delays too long, encourage him to think the symbols at once. Discuss his reactions and experience. Point out that his reaction to the symbol was the same when he gave it himself as when you gave it to him.

16. Now, you're going to hypnotize yourself. Simply make yourself comfortable, decide that you are going to hypnotize yourself (which is equivalent to giving permission to the hypnotist) and say, "Sleep, now!" Go ahead, hypnotize yourself.

Wait for the subject to display the obvious signs of response, and then resume.

94

17. Deeper and deeper, deeper and deeper. Your eyelids are sticking tightly closed. It is impossible for you to open them. Try to open them, try as hard as you can. It is impossible.

Wait for at least ten seconds, so that the subject can make an adequate test.

18. You see, it makes no difference who gives the signal. Your response is the same. Now, your eyelids are relaxed and normal. You could open them if you wished to, but please keep them closed. Will you please awaken yourself now?

Wait for the subject to awaken himself, and discuss the response with him. In working through the following verbal technique, make sure that he understands what you are doing, and repeats exactly.

19. Now, we are going to formulate a suggestion and symbolize it, so that you can produce your own response in hypnosis. Please repeat what I say. Repeat it aloud.

Such a formulation is done in the waking state always.

20. EYES is the symbol for the following suggestion. *(Wait for the subject to repeat aloud after you.)* My eyelids are locked tightly closed. *(Wait)*

My eyelid are locked so tight *(Wait)* that I cannot open them *(Wait)* no matter how hard I try *(Wait)*. I order my unconscious mind *(Wait)* to assume control of my eyelids *(Wait)*, and to keep them locked tight in spite of my conscious efforts to open them. *(Wait)* My eyelids are locked tight. *(Wait)* I cannot open them. *(Wait)* I cannot open them except by awakening myself *(Wait)* or by thinking the symbol "EYES OPEN." *(Wait)* This entire concept is symbolized *(Wait)* by the thought:

"EYES"

(Wait)

21. You have now formulated an order to yourself. It is unnecessary for you to think about the details of this suggestion. The procedure is very simple. Hypnotize yourself. When you feel the typical sensations of hypnosis, think the word EYES without any attempt to remember what it means. Then attempt to open your eyes. You will find them effectively and tightly closed. After you have tried to open them, and have satisfied yourself that it is impossible to do so, say the awakening signal, Wake up—one, two, three. Now, go ahead and try it.

Observe the subject's reaction as he hypnotizes himself, tests the eye catalepsy and awakens himself. Failures at this stage are rare. In the event that the eye catalepsy is not successful, discuss with him the possible reasons for it. Probable reasons for failure are (1) Attempting to remember what the symbol means; (2) Repeating the signal (symbol) over and over; (3) Trying to use the signal with great emphasis. A simple discussion of these possible causes of failure and the reassurance that he was simply "trying too hard" is usually sufficient to insure success on the second try. If the eyes open, but there was a noticeable difficulty in opening them, this fact may be pointed out to the subject, and he can be reassured that this evidence of some response shows that with a little practice he can acquire the knack of it.

22. Now formulate a suggestion without any assistance from me. Select some of the simple tests that we have used. Give yourself a verbal order worded about like the one we used for the eyes. Symbolize it. Say it aloud so that I can listen to it. Then hypnotize yourself, give the symbol, test it, and awaken yourself.

It is difficult to devise a word-for-word procedure from this point on. For further suggestions follow the rules of autohypnosis in Chapter V. A possible exception is the following formulation of a post-hypnotic suggestion:

23. Please repeat after me: "STUCK" is the symbol for the following suggestion. *(Wait)* When I am hypnotized I am going to clasp my hands together *(Wait)* like this *(illustrate by clasping hands, both subject and hypnotist)* and think, "Stuck!" *(Wait)* "Stuck" means that my hands are locked together. *(Wait)* My hands are clasped tightly together. *(Wait)* It is impossible for me to separate them, *(Wait)* now or after I awaken. *(Wait)* My hands are locked tightly together, *(Wait)* and will remain so until I stand up after I awaken. *(Wait)* The act of standing up *(Wait)* will release my hands *(Wait)* and return them to conscious control. *(Wait)* But nothing that I can do or say or think *(Wait)* will enable my hands to separate until I stand up. *(Wait)* My hands are locked tight together and will remain so even after I awaken *(Wait)* until I stand up. *(Wait)* This entire idea is symbolized by the thought

"STUCK"

(Wait)

24. Now, you have formulated a post-hypnotic suggestion for yourself. The procedure is: One, hypnotize yourself. Two, think "EYES." Three, test your eye catalepsy by trying to open them. When you cannot, you know that you are hypnotized, Four, clasp your hands together voluntarily. Five, think "STUCK." Six, try to separate your hands. You will find them locked together. Seven, wake yourself up with the signal, "Wake up—one, two, three." Eight, try to separate your hands. You will find that you have given yourself a very effective post-hypnotic suggestion. After you have tested this to your own satisfaction, Nine, stand up to release the catalepsy.

Make sure that the subject understands this series of steps, and then observe him carry them out. In some cases the post-hypnotic handclasp is not completely effective. In such cases point out previous experience with a completely successful hetero-suggested catalepsy. If necessary hypnotize subject and produce a completely effective post-hypnotic handclasp. Then have the subject repeat this procedure, after having given him strong suggestions while in hypnosis that his own orders to himself are just as, or even more, effective than the suggestions that you might give him. You will frequently find that subjects who have difficulty in accepting suggestions from you because of their fear of domination, will be able to accept these same suggestions much more readily when given by themselves to themselves.

The patient should be encouraged to practice these simple self-disciplines. It should be pointed out to him that while these serve no therapeutic purpose they bear the same relationship to therapeutic hypnosis as does the practicing of musical scales on an instrument to the rendition of beautiful music. The scales are a preliminary discipline.

The doctor who has mastered the various techniques given in this book will have no difficulty in helping his patient to formulate other practice suggestions.

CHAPTER XI

SUGGESTIVE THERAPY

Mr. T. had suffered a "back injury" when a streetcar stopped suddenly. After medical treatment had produced little improvement, he was referred for hypnotherapy with a diagnosis of traumatic neurosis. Mr. T. was receiving compensation and had little incentive to "get well" except for the "pain in his back." He proved unresponsive to the usual suggestions of sleep and to light trance tests. He did, however, achieve some degree of relaxation. Hypnoidal (that is, pre-hypnotic) suggestion was attempted.

He was seen three times a week. The procedure was to make him comfortable in a prone position, and then to talk relaxation while gently "rubbing" his back. The touch was very light, in no sense a massage. It was almost a caress and was used solely for its "soothing" qualities, and to direct the attention to the back.

During this period he was bombarded with suggestions of a positive nature. "Your back is getting stronger. Your back is getting stronger every day. You move freely and easily. Etc." At the end of two weeks he was persuaded to attempt to get about without the cane upon which he had been relying. At about that time a specific future time for him to return to work was selected by him, and suggestions were directed at that goal. After twelve sessions he was sent back to the referring physician, able to return to work.

99

HYPNOSIS AND SUGGESTION
FALSELY IDENTIFIED

Suggestive therapy has been identified with hypnotherapy since the time of Braid. So common was this misconception that Bernheim entitled his great book on medical hypnosis *"Suggestive Therapeutics."*[3] This false notion is still widespread, and must be guarded against.

SUGGESTION IN EVERYDAY LIFE

The physician uses suggestion in his practice consciously or unconsciously. For instance, a "bedside manner" is considered an asset to every general practitioner. A doctor who is skillful in gaining the confidence of a patient has won the first "round" against the illness. In the same class is the ability to imply (frequently without words) that all is well now that the doctor is in charge.

The foregoing are excellent examples of suggestion as used in the everyday life of the physician. They clarify the point that hypnosis need not be a part of suggestive therapy. Hypnosis is a modality, not a therapy.

HYPNOSIS MULTIPLIES THE
EFFECT OF SUGGESTION

Hypnosis strengthens and intensifies the effect of any suggestion. Hypnosis can be used to implement any verbal therapy.

CRITICISMS OF SUGGESTIVE THERAPY
NOT JUSTIFIED

The use of hypnosis with suggestion has been criticised many times. It has been called "symptom treatment." It has been described as temporary, and therefore useless. The reasoning behind such criticism is difficult to fathom. A physician who prescribes aspirin for a headache, or injects morphine to alleviate the sufferings of someone with a broken leg, is using supportive therapy. He knows that the aspirin or the morphine will nót cure the condition. But it gives relief, it helps the patient to endure the period during which more permanent results are being achieved.

The physician who uses suggestion to accomplish the same result is simply using a different modality, with this possible advantage: There are no physiological toxic effects from suggestion.

This advantage is offset to some degree by the fact that many doctors are not skillful hypnotists, and that many patients cannot be quickly and easily hypnotized. There can be no scientific or acceptable ethical reason for withholding the use of hypnosis when it can do a service to the patient. Arguments to the contrary remind one of the early opposition to the use of chloroform. At that time eminent physicians contended that "God meant man to feel pain."

LIMITATIONS AND DANGERS

It is necessary at this point to deal plainly with the one inherent danger of "symptom treatment." The danger is that it will be used blindly by a person who is unqualified to diagnose.

What can happen is this: a symptom might be alleviated while the cause of the symptom becomes more serious. Thus, it might be possible for an amateur hypnotist to "cure" the headache of someone who suffered from a brain tumor. Such a "cure" might delay a medical diagnosis until the malignancy had grown to a size where it could not be operated on successfully. The patient might die from a tumor which could have been diagnosed and surgically removed.

Or, again, an amateur might "cure" a stomach ache, and have his "patient" die of a ruptured appendix.

These possibiiities are conceivable. But then so is it conceivable that one of the many "doctor books" for the layman

101

will be used for diagnostic purposes, with the result that, when a doctor is finally called, the patient is dead or dying.

It is not possible to protect the foolish or the ignorant or (a very important element) the poverty-stricken from all the dangers of existence. There are people who have not yet learned to cross a street properly. We read their names in our daily papers.

DANGER FROM THE AMATEUR CAN
BE AVOIDED

The unqualified amateur hypnotist is not so great a hazard as might appear from the description of the extreme danger described in the foregoing. In the first place, even "symptom treatment" must usually be repeated at regular intervals before it "takes." This is not always the case. A good hypnotherapist can sometimes work wonders in one visit. But it is the rule rather than the exception that several treatments are necessary. (After all, the old complaint against hypnosis was that it did not provide a permanent cure.)

So, to begin with, the subject is protected from the fly-by-night hypnotist because permanency is nearly always the product of systematic treatment.

It has been the observation of the authors that the average individual who learns how to hypnotize uses it for a while, regarding it more or less as a toy. And then seldom or *never* uses it again. Few amateur hypnotists know how to handle a deep trance subject, how to train him, how to make use of his ability to be hypnotized. Even a good somnambulistic subject has to be handled with the proper verbal patterns, or he does not learn the techniques that it is possible for him to learn.

CAN THE LAY HYPNOTIST HELP?

Since this is a book which is designed to show the doctor how he can teach hypnotic response to his patients, so that

102

suggestive therapy will be more effective, it is important to indicate the way in which any danger can be best avoided. The method is extremely simple. The hypnotherapist should work in collaboration with a physician.

In its very simplest form this means that each patient should have a physical examination. He should find out what a competent general practitioner or specialist thinks lies at the root of the symptoms that are causing distress. If he can find no physical cause, then "symptom treatment" with hypnosis may be used. If one symptom vanishes and another one takes its place, then the cause is probably deeper, and the solution is psychotherapy, preferably with hypnosis because it is then faster and less expensve. (See also last Chapter).

GOOD SUGGESTION IS AN ART

With some patients, and under some conditions, the simple, flat statement of well-being is sufficient. Repeat "You are well!" many times, and the results are occasionally surprisingly good.

In general, however, more complicated suggestions must be used in order to produce results. The skillful formulation of a complicated suggestion is in itself an art requiring thought and ability on the part of the administering physician.

Fortunately, a systematic approach is possible. Suggestions are most effective when structured according to the first four rules as given in Chapter V.

LeCron and Bordeaux[21] have pointed out that a suggestion worded in a dynamic manner implying a transition from the present state of malaise to a future state of well-being is acceptable to the patient on an intellectual basis.

THE PATIENT HAS A
WILL TO BE WELL

Experience has shown that in deep trance the subject

tends to accept fully and literally any suggestion which produces a greater sense of well-being. The use of the future tense postpones his realization of the desired result to a vague and indefinite future time. The present tense is more powerful in its effect. This does not mean that a transitional state cannot be used. It can be. But the suggestion or process of therapy is incomplete unless it is carried through to the present tense.

SUGGESTION A STEP BY STEP
PROCESS

In gaining the acceptance of a therapeutical idea, it is frequently advisable to go through from one state to another. Let us take the example of the headache. We have taken a step forward if we first convince the subject that "it is possible to cure *a* headache through hypnosis."

Our next step must be to convince the subject that it is possible for *his* headache to be alleviated. When he has accepted that idea, and not before, he can be presented with the further statement that his headache is beginning to leave.

The positive method would, of course, be used. The words would not be, "Your headache is going away." They would be, "The muscles of your neck and scalp are relaxing. Your head is becoming clear, more and more clear. You are feeling better and better." And so on.

The next step is the positive, present tense suggestion. "Your head is clear, perfectly clear now." This can be reiterated for some time, after which comes the final time binding statement:

"Your head is clear now. It will be clear when you awaken. You are going to continue to be relaxed. Your head is clear now, and will stay clear from now on."

Please note that this latter sequence is an inter-mixture

of present and future. If such a binding of the present with the future does not take place, the suffering individual is confronted on the unconscious level with a curious conflict. "Your head is clear now," are the words that have been used up to the end of the present tense step. Now? When does "now" end?

Sometimes in a few minutes. Sometimes in an hour. Sometimes longer. But the conflict should be resolved with a definite pointing to the future, with the implication that "now" is forever.

CHAPTER XII

HYPNOTIC REEDUCATION

Mrs. F. was having marital difficulties. Her husband objected to certain normal social activities. She, in turn, objected to some of his behavior patterns. Both had received strict fundamental religious training in early childhood. Both had rigid ideas regarding "sin" and "right" and "wrong." The chief difficulty arose from the fact that their concepts did not agree. The early religions were different.

Both had moved on to other and more liberal religions, but the early training still influenced their thinking. Both proved to be responsive to hypnosis. Both received hypnotherapy in separate sessions, but the reeducation was parallel in structure.

The first step was to find out from each their individual attitude on God, heaven, hell, punishment, sin, etc. This was done in deep trance, and resulted in a satisfactory catharsis (verbal release of tension). Afterwards, while the patient was still in hypnosis, the psychologist read to each selected passages from "How Jesus Heals Our Minds Today" by David Seabury.[31] The post-hypnotic suggestion then followed. The suggestion was:

"I am reading to you from a very good book. You want to know more of this book. You are going to take this book home, and read it through from cover to cover. In reading this book, you will receive many new ideas to take the place of these old ideas which have been causing so much turmoil in your life. As you read the book, your ideas begin to change. By the time you have finished this book you and your (spouse) agree on these things and you live harmoniously and tranquilly together."

The book named is, of course, to be used only with people who would be willing to accept its ideas. For individuals who are non-religious (but whose problems are rooted in their early religious training) a different type of book would be more useful.

In the instance described the husband and wife read the book together. The hypnotic suggestion had opened their minds to the possibilities of. changing some of their previously fixed ideas. They became more tolerant and understanding not only of each other but also of their neighbors and friends. At subsequent therapeutic sessions the new ideas were reinforced.

THE AVERAGE PATIENT IS IGNORANT
OF HIS OWN PROBLEMS

People destroy themselves because they do not know any better. Ignorance and misconception are the common property of most patients with psychological or behavior problems. A large part of psychotherapy consists in helping the patient to unlearn that which he "knows"—*which is not so,* and helping him to learn that which he doesn't know (which is essential to his happiness) which *is so.* Hypnosis can accelerate the process of learning and unlearning.

WORDS ARE POTENT

In counselling or psychotherapy, words are the principal and frequently the only tools used. In both reading and listening, words are used to convey ideas. Each word carries some impact. Each word has an effect upon the nervous system. Each phrase or idea possesses a greater or lesser amount of "energy" depending upon the associations it arouses in a particular individual.

Let us imagine a person is standing behind a pillar and becoming aware that two acquaintances are standing on the other side of a pillar talking. He is about to reveal his presence when, suddenly, he realizes they are talking about him. The discovery electrifies him. He remains where he is, out of sight, in order to hear what they have to say.

At this point, as readers and students, let us draw back and consider what is about to happen. The eavesdropper is going to hear words. If he believes with the old Scottish proverb that "Sticks and stones may break my bones but words will never hurt me," then he will already be tensing against the possibility of critical remarks. Because that is the only way we can fool our conscious minds into believing that we don't really care. We must deny to ourselves that the words have any validity, or take a further step and cast doubt on the judgment of the person who utters them.

Actually, the "unconscious" mind will never forget anything that is said under the circumstances, whether the words are favorable or unfavorable.

Now, we are back at the pillar with the eavesdropper. His name is John, and he hears one of his acquaintances say, "John's all right but——" The other man agrees, adding, "Too bad he has B. O."

There we have the familiar advertisement situation, always effective and useful for many different products The millions of people who have reacted to such advertisements are a partial evidence that words are indeed powerful.

Now, let us imagine that the words heard by John were of a different nature. Suppose the first man had said, "John is the smartest man I know." If the second man agrees, then the effect will be uplifting. For days—actually years— John will be a happier, healthier man. Many things may happen to him. He may suffer serious reverses, but those favorable words cannot be unsaid. They will always weigh on the positive side and to his advantage even if he consciously forgets them.

In hypnosis, positive and beneficial words are the only ones that should be used.

HYPNOSIS INTENSIFIES THE IMPRESSION MADE BY EACH WORD

Each word we hear, then, has "energy" which can affect us for good or ill, depending on how we understand it, or in what circumstances we receive it. In order to comprehend how hypnosis effects that "energy," let us compare our words to a radio broadcasting station which continually emits a certain amount of energy.

If we erect an aerial and connect to that aerial a simple one-tube radio set, we will intercept some of that radiated energy. It will activate the earphones of the radio set and we will hear a small volume of sound.

We have now the equivalent of words affecting us without hypnosis.

But we quickly add to our set three stages of amplification and a loudspeaker. Immediately, there is an increased volume of sound. There has been no change, please note, in the input of energy. The aerial is still intercepting the same amount of energy, but the output is much greater.

Hypnosis should be considered as the amplifying circuit which may be added to any verbal therapy. Any word that can favorably affect a particular individual's nervous system can be amplified by the technique of hypnosis to produce a much greater effect.

SIMPLE DISCUSSION IS EFFECTIVE

If the patient has learned to be hypnotized, hypnotize him and give him the information that he needs while he is in hypnosis. This use of hypnosis may be distinguished from suggestive therapy in that objective information is being imparted to the patient rather than a subjective experience suggested.

Frequently, the doctor will have an adequate speaking knowledge of the subject under discussion. In this event, he can tutor the hypnotized patient. No special verbal formulations are necessary in utilizing hypnotic reeducation as a therapy. When it is discovered that the patient has been badly misinformed in a certain field of behavior, or has strong guilt feelings about experiences or attitudes which are normal and natural, specific information about the behavior of other people will often work wonders, without as well as with hypnosis.

BIBLIOTHERAPY

In our culture reading is the predominant method of acquiring higher level learning. More primitive methods, of course, are listening in order to acquire the second-hand experience of others, and actual life experiences which give first-hand learning.

The doctor will find the printed word one of his most valuable allies. In many cases it will be found helpful to read to the hypnotized patient passages from books which give the necessary information. Authoritative books carry a prestige value which can add to the prestige of the therapist and help him to gain quick acceptance of ideas which may be new to the patient or even be opposed to his previous concepts.

Physicians who use bibliotherapy as an habitual procedure are advised to be well acquainted with the books they lend or recommend. Such books usually contain an essential idea which is presented in numerous ways in certain passages. The physician who is familiar with these passages can read them to the patient either with or without hypnosis.

The objection to bibliotherapy without hypnosis is that it imparts information on intellectual levels without reaching the emotional level where changes in attitude are produced. By definition, hypnosis deals with emotional effects. The same words read to the patient in deep hypnosis produce a far more profound emotional effect than if read by or to the patient in the waking state.

ADDITIONAL SUGGESTIVE THERAPY
WITH HYPNOSIS BENEFICIAL

Hypnotic reeducation in itself will in many cases produce changes in emotional attitudes. In other cases, where the information given failed to dispel guilt feelings or anxiety, the reeducation can be used as a foundation for suggestive therapy. Having read authoritative passages describing the conduct of others, one may say to the patient, "You are normal. You react normally. These thoughts and feelings and actions, of which you have been so ashamed, or about which you have felt so guilty, or which have created so much anxiety, are normal and natural. Now that you know that these actions are normal, you feel emotionally free. Now that you know these thoughts are normal, you feel like other people, etc."

SEMANTICS AND HYPNOSIS
CAN BE JOINED

Students of the work of Alfred Korzybski[18] have made use use of hypnosis in teaching "general semantics" to patients taking psychological training. As Korzybski points out, an intellectual understanding of maturity does not bring maturity. Many erudite and highly intelligent people are consistently infantile in their emotional reactions and behavior patterns. This is very confusing to the average person and is one of the reasons why intellectualism is so often held in contempt.

It is fairly easy to gain intellectual knowledge of the way the human body and mind as a whole should function if it were mature. It is much more difficult to train an individual's nervous system to function in a mature manner.

111

A METHOD FOR TEACHING SEMANTICS
IN HYPNOSIS

Wilbur E. Moore[27] has presented an interesting study of the use of hypnosis in the cure of stuttering through the hypnotic teaching of the principles of "general semantics." Others have used similar methods in teaching the mechanics of discrimination and of non-identification to people with emotional problems.

One method is to give the subject a post-hypnotic suggestion about as follows: "I have a book which can teach you a method of solving your own problems. I am going to lend you this book. You will learn valuable methods of judgment and discrimination by reading it. Take it home with you. Read it carefully. Study it. When you are through with it, bring it back, and we will discuss it."

The patient is then lent Lee,[22] Hayakawa,[12] Johnson[16] or Korzybski,[18] depending on the education and personality of the individual. Such a post-hypnotic suggestion carries more weight than a simple recommendation of the book. The patient as a rule reads the book rather swiftly, and in the reading acquires an intellectual understanding of some of the processes. He becomes acquainted with the terminology.

When he finally returns the book, he is hypnotized and the contents are discussed with him. Certain portions of the book are then read back to him, and finally he is given powerful suggestions to react in that way. In the terminology of the general semanticist, the subject is conditioned to have a "signal reaction" of a "delayed reaction." Or, as Pavlov might say it, we establish in the subject a conditioned reflex to make mature judgments, to discriminate.

To anyone who understands its significance, this will surely seem one of the great possibilities of hypnotic reeducation.

CHAPTER XIII

INSOMNIA

The inability to sleep soundly is usually a symptom of anxiety. Where it has been established that sleeplessness has no definite physiological cause, hypnosis will in many cases produce satisfactory relief.

All the techniques of depth analysis or psychotherapy are sometimes necessary to produce a personality change which will eliminate the anxiety, of which insomnia will normally be but one of several symptoms. The doctor who is qualified to undertake such analysis will occasionally find it advisable to do so, or else to refer his patient to a psychologist or psychiatrist.

While deep analysis is sometimes advisable, it is not essential to the removal of the symptom of insomnia. On the other hand, a few questions may bring out the cause of the anxiety. Where this is possible, a purely "symptom treatment" with hypnotic suggestion may result in a permanent "cure."

FOR THE DOCTOR

Hypnotize patient as deeply as possible, the deeper the better. Light trance, however, will frequently produce desired results.

As a baby you slept when you needed sleep. As a child

113

you slept when you needed sleep. It is possible for you to regain that ability, to slumber comfortably under any conditions of comfort, in any environment no matter how noisy or light, and regardless of your emotional condition at the time of going to sleep.

You know mature people who can go to sleep instantly at any time. It is possible for you to go to sleep instantly and easily.

You are going to learn to go to sleep. You are going to learn to go to sleep instantly. You are going to learn to go to sleep in any physical position. You are going to learn to go to sleep in any surroundings. You are going to learn to go to sleep in noisy surroundings. You are going to learn to go to sleep with light shining on your face or in darkness. You are going to learn to sleep soundly. You are going to learn to sleep so soundly that nothing but an emergency can disturb you. You are going to learn to awaken instantly when wakefulness is necessary, and then to return to sleep easily and quickly. You are going to learn to sleep as long as you wish to. You are going to learn to awaken at the time you select.

You are now learning to sleep soundly and deeply. You are deeply hypnotized and going deeper. You have learned to be hypnotized at a signal. You have formed the habit of going to sleep when I give the signal.

Tonight there will come a time when you will want to go to bed. Go through your usual routine, if you have one. It doesn't really matter—I mention it so that you will know that there are no restrictions being placed on your normal way of living. You can approach the bedtime hour in any way you please, by following a routine or by not following a routine.

However, when you finally crawl between the sheets, and close your eyes with the intention of going to sleep, you

114

begin the new and simple routine of easy slumber. Take a very deep breath and exhale it.

Wait for inhalation.

As you exhale, your body relaxes as it is now relaxed. Take a second and deeper breath.

Wait for inhalation.

Exhale it slowly. As you exhale this breath you sink deeper and deeper into hypnosis, deeper than you are now, breathing slowly and gently. Within two minutes you pass from hypnosis into a deep and restful slumber. Is that pattern all right with you?

Wait for nod.

Very well, that's the way it is. Remember, tonight when you finally crawl into bed to sleep, you inhale a very deep breath, and as you exhale your whole body relaxes. You take a second and deeper breath and as you exhale slowly that is the signal for you to go into hypnosis. From hypnosis you pass into a deep and restful slumber, and you have the most comfortable and satisfying night's rest that you have ever experienced. You slumber undisturbed through the entire night unless an emergency should occur. Emergencies are very rare, but just in case something does happen which makes it necessary for you to get out of bed, you awaken instantly and alertly, do what is necessary, and then go back to bed and slumber soundly through the rest of the night. You awaken at your usual hour in the morning, or at any time which you have previously selected for awakening, and it is the most cheerful and vigorous awakening of your entire life. All through tomorrow your energy remains at a high level; and from now on every time you go to bed by this method you find that slumber comes quickly and is undisturbed and restful. All through tomorrow your energy remains at a high level; and from now on every time you go to bed by this method you find that slumber comes quickly and is continuous and restful. From now on every time you go to bed by this method you will find that slumber comes quickly and is undisturbed and restful. From now on every time you go to bed by this method slumber comes quickly and is continuous and restful. From now on every time you go to bed by this method slumber comes quickly and is undisturbed and restful. The habit of natural slumber is completely re-established.

FOR THE PATIENT

The following autohypnotic formulation is to be read aloud by the patient before retiring. The symbol will be the hour of awakening. (Hour) is used as the symbol in this formulation. The patient must understand that where (Hour) is used, he is to say "6:30," "8," "7:45," etc. This construction gives flexibility to the suggestion.

(Hour) is the symbol for the following suggestion: Two minutes after thinking (Hour), I pass from the hypnotic sleep into deep, sound, restful, natural slumber. One hundred and twenty seconds after thinking (Hour), I pass from hypnosis into a restful, relaxed, peaceful, natural sleep. I sleep deeply and continuously throughout the night. I sleep restfully and with complete relaxation. I sleep soundly and continuously unless there is some real and necessary reason for me to awaken. If there is such a necessity, I awaken instantly, clear-headed, alert, and ready to do what is necessary. When this is done, and I return to my bed, I again return to sleep within two minutes. There is little chance of such a necessity and, barring such a chance, I sleep continuously throughout the night. The normal noises of the night go on, and I am oblivious to them. I sleep soundly through the normal noises of the night. I sleep continuously and with perfect relaxation. I awaken promptly at (Hour), rested, rejuvenated, and filled with energy and pep. I awaken promptly at (Hour) happy, refreshed, and ready to enjoy the coming day. I

116

awaken promptly at (Hour), cheerful, alert and ready to get up.

This whole idea is symbolized by the thought: (Hour).

INSTRUCTIONS FOR
THE PATIENT

Copy this suggestion on a card or paper. Have it available at bedtime. Read the suggestion to yourself aloud. If you do not wish others to know you are giving yourself the suggestion, you can whisper it. But it is important to bring into use as much of the nervous system as possible. After reading the suggestion, dismiss it from your mind. When you get into bed, and have assumed your usual sleeping position, hypnotize yourself. After testing your hypnotic response by one of the simple tests, such as eye catalepsy, think (Hour) once, lightly. Make NO effort to remember the suggestion that you read to yourself, to keep track of the time, or to repeat the symbol. Deliberately engage your mind in pleasant reverie or fantasy after you have given yourself the symbol.

REMEMBER: "The greater the conscious effort, the less the unconscious response." And vica versa. By thinking the symbol once only, you are using an absolute minimun of conscious effort. If this does not work, it is because you are "trying too hard." Read the suggestion aloud once more, rehypnotize yourself, and repeat the whole procedure. This time TAKE IT EASY

NOTE TO DOCTOR

The above formulation can also be used as a hetero-hypnotic suggestion by asking the patient what time he wishes to arise the next morning, and then reading the whole suggestion to the patient substituting "you" for "I," and eliminating the words "from the hypnotic sleep" and "from hypnosis."

117

For your convenience, underline the words that are either to be eliminated or changed.

CASE HISTORIES

i

Dr. T., in his sixties, and practically retired, suffered from persistent insomnia of many years standing. He proved to be a light trance subject the first time hypnosis was attempted, and in the course of several one-hour sessions developed a medium trance response. Simple post-hypnotic suggestions such as the hand clasp were successful. During this period of time his conversation revealed many other anxiety symptoms. Dr. T. had accepted self-consciousness, stage fright, and feelings of inferiority as part of his personality structure. He manifested no interest in facing these problems but was eager to recapture the ability to go to sleep quickly, and to sleep soundly.

Because of the doctor's age and his lack of interest in facing the problems of his total personality it was decided to concentrate on the insomnia in an attempt at symptom relief. After six hourly sessions of training in hypnotic response, the doctor was conditioned in auto-hypnosis in a one-hour session. The suggestion under the "For the Patient" heading in this chapter was dictated to the doctor. It was regarded as an important detail that the doctor write this suggestion rather than be handed a typed or printed copy. He was instructed in the use of the suggestion and sent home to try it.

The first night it was unsuccessful. At the next session the doctor was cautioned "not to try too hard," to exert a minimum of cortical activity, to think the key word once and only once, to think it lightly and without effort. That night the doctor was successful, and has since reported an unbroken record of success. He now goes to sleep at will within two or three minutes, and sleeps soundly.

A similar but contrasting case is that of the retired contractor, Mr. C., also in his late sixties. Mr. C. obtained a high degree of relaxation in his first attempt at hypnosis, but failed on all tests. He was considered to be in the hypnoidal state. Because of the nature of the patient's personality, it was decided to use hypnoidal suggestion (in an attempt to teach a specific conditioning) rather than try to teach him a more generalized autohypnosis which could also be used for other purposes. Starting with the second session, a simple relaxing technique was used until Mr. C's eyes closed, and he achieved an obvious muscular relaxation of the entire body. At that time the following brief and simple suggestion was given:

"Tonight when you are in bed and ready to go to sleep, think to yourself, 'So sleepy, so sleepy, so sleepy.' Then let your mind drift. These words remind you of the way you feel right now, and you will begin to feel this way. Within two minutes you go to sleep. You sleep deeply and restfully all night long. You awaken when you want to awaken, feeling refreshed and ready to get up."

This suggestion was repeated over and over for an hour. Mr. C. did as he was told that night, lay awake for two hours and finally took his usual sedative. The following day the entire procedure was repeated, including Mr. C's failure to sleep until he took a sedative. After the seventh daily session, Mr. C. jubilantly reported success. The conditioning was continued for five more sessions. There were no failures after the first success. As an interesting by-product of this training, he was tested for eye catalepsy at the end of the twelfth hour. It was effective. Mr. C. had learned to go into a light trance. On the other hand, slightly more complicated suggestions (such as heavy or rigid arm) were not successful.

After a few months of successful sleep induction, Mr. C. commented that he had changed the signals to himself. He said, "When I lie down and close my eyes, I erect a wall on either side of my thoughts. Then I bring these walls together until they will let me go in only one direction. Then I mentally sort of shout 'SLEEP!' And I'm gone."

Fourteen months later Mr. C. requested hypnotherapy on another matter. He was asked to hypnotize himself while holding the thought that he would be responsive to the hypnotist's suggestions. As the relaxation developed, the usual routine of suggestions were used for deepening of trance. This was followed by a routine series of tests. Mr. C. responded to every test, including post-hypnotic suggestions and total amnesia. In fourteen months of light autohypnotic practice he had taught himself to be a deep trance subject.

Almost four years have passed since the original hypnoidal therapy. Mr. C. is still in perfect control of his sleeping habits and is still a deep trance subject.

CHAPTER XIV

HEADACHE

As with insomnia, headache is frequently a symptom of anxiety. In such cases a casual analysis may bring out the cause of the anxiety, but more often deep analysis is required.

It is possible to relieve headache with direct suggestion, using hypnosis, and even the lightest trance is sometimes adequate. Where there is response to suggestions for general relaxation, some relief may be looked for. Like many symptoms, headaches can be eliminated in some cases without any analysis whatsoever. With prolonged treatment, this has been successfully applied to severe cases of migraine, where the cause was not physical pathology.

FOR THE DOCTOR

Ask the subject exactly where the pain seems to be localized. Then hypnotize subject to light trance or deeper.

Now, you are relaxing more completely than ever before. You are going deeper and deeper to sleep, relaxing more and more. Every muscle in your body is relaxing, and will continue to relax more with every breath that you take. You are letting go. Your muscles are letting go. You are becoming loose and limp and lazy.

Reinforce the following suggestions with a gentle massage. Touch while you are talking, and in the places you are talking about.

121

Now we are going to make your head feel free and clear. Now, all these muscles in the neck are letting go even more. They are becoming loose and flexible. The muscles are becoming loose and flexible, like rubber bands tossed loosely on the desk. The neck muscles are relaxing more and more and more. Now, the base of the skull is becoming completely relaxed, loose, limp. You are beginning to feel so good, you are feeling better and better and better. *(Repeat foregoing sentence many times.)* Now, your forehead and temples are relaxing, letting go, letting go. The muscles are relaxing and you are feeling so much better, so very much better. *(Repeat many times.)*

By now your head should be feeling very, very good, but just to make sure that you feel absolutely perfect when you awaken, we'll work a little on the exact spot.

Place hand on the area previously indicated by patient.

Now, as I hold my hand here, you are feeling more and more perfect, more and more perfect. Your head is becoming clear and perfect. You are feeling emotionally serene and perfect. As I take my hand away, you will notice that your head is absolutely clear and perfect, clear and perfect. You feel wonderful. You feel absolutely perfect.

Remove hand quickly.

Now, your head feels perfect, clear and perfect, and it is going to continue to feel that way after you awaken and for the rest of the day. Your head is going to continue to feel more and more perfect after you awaken and for the rest of the day.

Use vigorous suggestions for well-being for waking signal. After the subject is awakened, question him about his feelings. The response is usually, "It's all gone. I feel wonderful." Occasionally, the reply will be, "It's better," and sometimes there is no difference. Even in the latter case it is well to remind the patient that it sometimes takes an ap-

*preciable length of time for a suggestion to become fully
effective. In 15 or 20 minutes the headache may be gone.*

FOR THE PATIENT

*Self-induced and self-controlled anaesthesias can be
taught the medium or deep trance subject with a minimum
of effort. Light trance subjects require longer training.
But anaesthesias also seem possible for them. In any case,
where self-induced anaesthesia is to be taught, it is advisable to use the glove anaesthesia as an introduction. Direct
prestige suggestions for anaesthesia of a chronic pain sometimes fail because of the overwhelming weight of previous
experience on the part of the patient. When, on the other
hand, an educational anaesthesia has been induced in a
neutral area, such as the hand, the patient has the positive
effect of his own experience. His reaction is then based,
not on "blind belief" in what you say, but a belief in his own
experience.*

*If the patient has had previous experience with the symp-
tom removal of a headache through the doctor's suggestion,
the patient may be given a cue or symbol to produce the
same effect.*

*Relieve the headache by using the hetero-hypnotic tech-
nique, but do not use the suggestions for continued well-
being. In other words, do not make the relief a post-hypnotic suggestion. Proceed:*

Now that your head is perfectly clear, and feels wonderful, we are going to teach you how this headache can be
controlled. We've just sent it away, and your head feels
perfect now, doesn't it? *(Wait)* Now we are going to bring
it back. Now your head is beginning to feel more and more
as it felt before. Now your head is aching more and more.
Soon, it will be aching worse than when you came in. We
will wait for a little while, and as soon as you feel the head-

ache to be worse than it was before, you lift your hand to your head.

Wait for the suggestion to take effect. When the subject lifts his hand to his head, continue.

Now we are going to make your head feel free and clear, just as we did before. This time *your* hand is on the head, instead of mine. And as you hold your hand there, your muscles are relaxing, and your head is becoming clear and free, just as it did before, but very much faster, very much faster. Your head is becoming clear and perfect. When *you* take *your* hand away, you will notice that your head is absolutely clear and perfect, clear and perfect.

Wait for the hand to be removed.

You feel wonderful, just as you felt when I relieved it. Now, we are going to arrange a signal that will remind you of this entire experience. The signal is the word "CLEAR."

The next time you have a headache, simply hold your hand to your head and say aloud the word "CLEAR." When you say that word, you will automatically be reminded of everything that happened here this time. You will be reminded of the words that I have said, and you will automatically feel just as you feel now, and even better. It is very simple. You have nothing to do but put your hand to your head and say the word "CLEAR." Hold your hand there a few seconds—or minutes—and then take your hand away. By the time your hand leaves, your head will be perfectly clear, and you will feel perfect. This signal will work just as well if I use it. If you should ever have a headache, all that is necessary is that either you or I place a hand on the head where the ache is, say the word "CLEAR," and after a little while take the hand away. During this time, the muscles relax, and the head becomes perfect in feeling.

Occasionally, with a deep trance subject, one or two applications of this technique will give the patient a degree of control over psychosomatic headaches, and in many cases

124

will enable the patient to block a referred pain from an organic disorder. In other cases, numerous repetitions of this educational procedure must be made before the subject "gets the knack of it."

CASE HISTORY

Occasionally the mere induction of hypnosis with its accompanying physical and emotional relaxation will produce a spontaneous and unexpected relief for a headache. This was well illustrated on one occasion when a psychologist was testing the efficiency of a "hypnotizing machine." The subjects were unaware that they were to be hypnotized. Prehypnotic suggestion was given to the subjects in a disguised form. They were asked to read a page of typewritten copy which was presented as a "rough draft of the advertising material that we are going to use with this machine." Each subject was asked to give an opinion of the clarity and understandability of the "advertising material." Actually, the "advertising matter" told them exactly what would happen to them as the result of their contact with the machine.

Some twenty-five subjects were hypnotized in this way. The degree of response was evaluated by the subject's comment on the sense of physical well-being after awakening.

One woman, upon awakening, said in surprise, "Oh, my headache is gone!" In response to questionings, she stated that periodically she experienced migraine headaches, and that one had started some time previous to this "relaxation." For the previous hour the pain had been increasing in intensity. During the relaxation, the headache disappeared. It did not return that day or the next.

The psychologist never saw this woman again. It is highly improbable that the single hypnotic session did anything of lasting value for her. The case is presented simply as an example of the way in which a headache may be eliminated without any direct suggestion toward that end.

Simple tension headaches frequently respond to light hypnosis or even waking suggestion. As an example of how casually this can be done, at a social gathering this psychologist noticed that one of the party had withdrawn herself. On being questioned, she admitted having a headache. This women had never been hypnotized and, since she did not desire to be the center of attention, it was not possible to attempt any usual hypnotic technique. The psychologist stepped behind her and said, "Let me fix that up for you. Just lean your head back in your chair, close your eyes, and let your body get as limp as possible."

He then massaged her forehead, the temples, the back of the neck and the shoulders for several minutes. He added nothing to the previous simple suggestion. When he noticed an increase in the relaxation, he simply patted her briskly on the shoulder and stepped away with the question: "How is it now?" Her surprised answer was, "Why, it's gone." The headache did not return that evening.

CHAPTER XV

CONSTIPATION

Hypnosis may be used effectively to alleviate constipation whether or not the problems of the particular individual are of psychosomatic origin. The case history described in detail immediately after the word-for-word general therapy for constipation is an excellent example of the use of hypnosis to help a boy suffering from congenital megacolon.

However, the attending doctor in more "normal" cases of constipation might well think in terms of certain types of early childhood training. The baby does not distinguish between the various pleasures it experiences during its first year. The joy of eating, the relief of urination and defecation are part of life. The mother has a different outlook. There comes the time, usually too early, when the mother attempts to train the child to "use the potty." Some children, when they discover that giving feces brings praise, immediately start a pattern of giving.

During the early part of the training period, the baby does not know what is expected of it. The baby continues to defecate and urinate on impulse and without regard to time or place. The mother adopts a firm attitude. A painful slap is sometimes administered, words like "Nasty" and "Dirty" are freely used, and by the time the baby "gets the idea," a connection has been established in its nervous system between the words, the act, and the organs involved.

One child discovers how eager the mother is for an habitual movement, and holds back to spite the parent. Another child, confused by the sharp words, holds back out of fear that his bowel movements offend no matter where they are delivered.

In using hypnosis to relieve constipation, the childhood experiences can usually be overcome without it being necessary to explain the possible causes to the patient. But if the problem does not yield readily to the hypnotic word-for-word technique that follows, it might be advisable to explore the back history and explain to the patient some of the unconscious processes that lie behind constipation.

It should be noted that a daily bowel movement is by no means a universal requirement. For some people twice, or even once a week is normal. The hypnotist should avoid changing the basic habit patterns of the individual's body functions.

FOR THE DOCTOR

Hypnotize the patient to the light trance stage or deeper.

Go deeper and deeper to sleep. Deeper and deeper to sleep. Much deeper and deeper to sleep. As you go deeper, your body is relaxing more and more, more and more. Now, your lips are beginning to relax. They are becoming loose and limp and flexible, and the jaw muscles are relaxing, so that your teeth do not quite touch. The throat muscles are relaxing, relaxing more and more. Now a wave of relaxation is starting down the esophagus towards your stomach.

Go deeper and deeper to sleep. Deeper and deeper to sleep. You know that your whole gastro-intestinal system is simply a muscular tube which is coiled round and round inside your body. Various parts of this tube have various purposes, just like the specialized departments in a factory. The mouth is the receiving department, where goods are accepted and unpacked. The throat and esophagus are the conveyor system. The stomach is a processing room in which the materials are prepared for use, and so on throughout the whole system. And finally we have the useful products which go into the body itself, and the waste products which we must eliminate.

This whole factory has a continuous conveyor system. The tubes which make up this conveyor system are composed of rings of muscles. These muscles in their contractions and relaxation push the material along through the factory just like the assembly line chain in an automobile factory. When we start the relaxation at the throat, that is automatically followed by the natural rhythmic alternate relaxation and contraction of the muscle. These contractions occur in waves always traveling from the receiving room down toward the waste disposal departments.

The wave of relaxation, which we started a few minutes ago, in the mouth and throat, is now moving down through the stomach towards the duodenum. Following the wave of relaxation come the peristaltic waves—alternate relaxation and contraction of the muscles, down through the stomach, the duodenum, and into the intestine. Your whole intestinal tract is becoming relaxed, and soon these waves will reach through the colon to the rectum. The rectum is a kind of storage bin, just like a waste basket. We don't run to empty a waste basket every time we get something in it. We do empty it when it gets full.

That is the way your body functions, too. These peristaltic waves carry the waste material through the colon and into the rectum where it is stored. As soon as it becomes full, an automatic signal is sent out, and you realize you are about to have a bowel movement. As soon as you have that feeling, you go to the toilet. When you sit down on the toilet, the contact of your body with the toilet seat automatically sends a signal to the round muscle which keeps the waste valve closed the rest of the time. This round muscle we call the sphincter. The waste valve we call the anus.

When you sit down on the toilet, the sphincter muscle relaxes. It becomes soft and flexible and stretches easily. And these waves of muscular contraction in the colon and rectum force the material out. These waves are working on down through your intestines now. And soon after you leave here you will feel the urge to have a bowel movement. When you feel this urge, go to the toilet, sit down and wait. Make no effort. Your body will take care of that part automatically and without effort. Make absolutely no effort. Your body can dispose of its waste material perfectly, if you do not interfere. Make no effort at all. Simply sit on the toilet and wait. The act of sitting on the toilet will be a signal to your unconscious mind. The sphincter muscle will relax. The rectum will empty itself easily and automatically.

Every time you eat, your jaws automatically tense and relax. Eating is an automatic signal which starts the entire process in motion. You eat. Your throat swallows the food, alternately relaxing and contracting. The wavelike action proceeds all through your stomach, duodenum and intestines. Soon after eating, you feel the urge to go to the toilet. Soon after eating, you feel the urge to go to the toilet. When you feel the urge, you go. The act of sitting on the toilet is automatically a signal to the sphincter muscle. It relaxes. The muscle relaxes. There is no effort on your part. The whole process is automatic. When you eat, the relaxation starts. Soon after eating, you experience the urge to go to the toilet. You go to the toilet. You go to the toilet immediately when you feel the urge. When you sit on the toilet, that is automatically a signal for the anus to relax and become soft and flexible. Then the rectum automatically empties itself. There is nothing for you to do consciously but go to the toilet when you feel the urge. All the rest happens automatically and naturally.

130

Shortly after you awaken, you are going to have the urge to go to the toilet. When you have that urge, go. And you will have an easy, natural bowel movement. Every time you eat, it is automatically the start of the process that will bring about an easy, natural, bowel movement. When you have the urge to go to the toilet, go immediately. Your body will take care of the rest. You are going to have a bowel movement shortly after you awaken, and you will have another one after your next meal.

FOR THE PATIENT

Auto-hypnotic formulations can provide a frequent reinforcement of the suggestion given by the doctor. The patient who has successfully responded to the hetero-hypnotic technique printed on the preceding pages, may be given the following suggestion for "homework."

EASY is the symbol for the following suggestion:

Every time I eat a meal I start the natural process which ends in an easy, natural bowel movement. When I start to chew and swallow, the alternate waves of relaxation and contraction carry on down through my entire intestinal system. By the time I finish eating, my body is proceeding in a natural and easy way toward a perfect elimination. Eating is the signal for me to have a bowel movement soon after the meal is finished. When I eat breakfast, I arise from the table with the urge to have a bowel movement. When I go to the toilet, the act of sitting on the toilet relaxes the round muscles, and without effort I have an easy natural bowel movement. When I eat lunch, I arise from the table with the urge to have a bowel movement. When I go to the toilet, the act of sitting on the toilet relaxes the round muscles and without effort I have an easy, natural bowel movement. When I eat dinner (or supper), I arise from the table with the urge to have a bowel movement. When I go to the toilet, the act of sitting on the toilet relaxes the round muscles,

131

and without effort I have an easy, natural bowel movement. Every time I have an easy natural bowel movement, it makes the habit stronger. Each time it makes the habit of easy, natural bowel movement stronger.

This whole idea is symbolized by the thought

EASY

INSTRUCTIONS FOR THE PATIENT

Copy this suggestion on a card or paper. Read it to yourself aloud. Hypnotize yourself. Test the hypnosis (with an eye catalepsy or hand levitation). Think the symbol once lightly. Let your mind flow in reverie or fantasy for a few minutes while the suggestion is "sinking in." Awaken yourself, much relaxed and refreshed. Give no conscious thought to the suggestion or its meaning except when you are reading it aloud. Avoid thinking of the suggestion while you are eating or when going to the toilet. Give yourself the suggestion at least once a day, if possible, two or three times daily.

CASE HISTORY

Some of the possibilities of the use of suggestion in correcting gastro-intestinal malfunction are illustrated by the following case.

Johnny had never experienced a natural, unaided bowel movement. That portion of his nervous system which should have produced a normal muscular contraction was defective at birth. He suffered from congenital megacolon.

At age 18 months, a sympathectomy was performed in an effort to achieve a balance in nervous control of the bowel. This operation was not successful in giving him the ability to move his bowels naturally. His childhood was normal except for the unceasing round of visits to the hospital for colonic irrigation and the constant search for a physician who "might be able to do something."

When he was twelve, his parents heard of Dr. X, who was giving a great deal of attention to the psychosomatic side of medicine. Dr. X combined the usual medical therapies with diets and hypnotherapy. He hypnotized Johnny and gave him strong positive suggestions that the bowels would move naturally. Shortly thereafter, Johnny had his first unaided bowel movement. A program of therapy was then undertaken, and very shortly the hypnotherapy was referred to a psychologist. Johnny continued to receive medication and diet supervision from the busy physician while the psychologist handled the more time-consuming hypnotic re-education. Within three months, Johnny was having three or four natural bowel movements a week. During the first month, he was hypnotized three times a week. Thirty minutes of each trance period were devoted to giving Johnny a "good time." He was given the illusion of participating in airplane flights, etc. (See Chapter XXI on Working with Children.) This was found necessary because in the course of 12 years, Johnny had become slightly "allergic" to doctors' offices. He begrudged the time spent there, which was of course taken from his play-time, rarely from school or chores. After school started, it proved especially difficult to convince Johnny that it was "all worth-while." But the hypnotic analysis of the relationship between physical health, success in sports, and personal popularity gave him the incentive to continue. After six months of therapy, the psychologist suggested to Johnny's father that the reading of a technique might produce effective results if done at home by the father or mother.

Johnny was taught to hypnotize himself. A suggestion was then prepared. Every night at bedtime, Johnny was to hypnotize himself, and his father or mother was to read the suggestion to him.

(The word-for-word suggestion given to Johnny follows after the next paragraph.)

A year after the start of the therapy, Johnny was allowed to go to a boy scout camp. He won the medal for excellence in swimming, and in general was one of the outstanding boys. On returning home, he reported that he had had a natural bowel movement *every day*. At present, he goes to the hospital for a colonic irrigation about every two weeks, and has a natural bowel movement almost every day.

The following is the word-for-word conditioning used with Johnny, whose problem was congenital megacolon. Johnny was trained to hypnotize himself. The technique was read to him by his father or mother each night when he went to bed.

Please close your eyes, Johnny, and hypnotize yourself. *(Wait for eyes to close and the appearance of relaxation.)* You are going deeper and deeper to sleep. Deeper and deeper to sleep. As soon as I stop talking to you, you will be sound asleep, sound asleep. You sleep perfectly tonight. You sleep perfectly tonight. If any gas forms, you roll over on your side as Dr. X showed you and get rid of the gas without even awakening. You do this automatically in your sleep. You sleep restfully and peacefully all night long, and tomorrow morning you awaken promptly at (———) o'clock full of pep and energy, all ready to get up and have a wonderful day.

You awaken with a good appetite and enjoy a fine breakfast. Right after breakfast you go to your room and expel the gas if there is any. Every day there is less gas. Soon, there will be no gas, but when there is any, you get rid of it. That makes you full of pep and energy for your day at school. You feel wonderful and at noon you have a good appetite for lunch. Eating lunch automatically starts your bowels working. When you finish lunch you feel that your bowels are all ready to move. You go to the toilet and have

134

a big, healthy, easy, natural bowel movement. You have an easy, natural bowel movement every day right after lunch. You have a bowel movement every day. You have a bowel movement every day. Every time your bowels move, the muscles grow stronger. Every time your bowels move, the muscles grow stronger. The nerves leading to the bowels are growing stronger and stronger. The nerves are growing stronger. Every time your bowels move they grow stronger. Every time your bowels move they grow stronger. Each movement makes the next one easier. Every time your bowels move the next movement comes easier. Your bowels are getting stronger and stronger.

After your bowel movement you feel fine. You feel fine all day. At dinner time you have a good appetite. You eat a good dinner and you thoroughly enjoy it. You enjoy your dinner. You have lots of fun during the evening, and at bedtime you are all ready to have another night of perfect sleep. Now, you are about to go to sleep. As you sleep, your body is growing stronger. The nerves are growing stronger. The muscles are growing stronger. Your bowels are growing strong and perfect, strong and perfect. Your bowels are growing strong and perfect. When I stop talking you will be sound asleep. Don't bother to answer me when I say goodnight. Just go deeper and deeper to sleep. Sleep perfectly until (———) o'clock. Wake up at (———) o'clock feeling full of pep and energy. Sleep perfectly. Good night. Sleep perfectly. Sleep perfectly. Sleep perfectly.

CHAPTER XVI

REDUCING

Generally speaking, hypnosis can be used to help those people who are overweight because they eat too much. There are reasons why people eat more than they need, and hypnotic re-education as well as suggestion with hypnosis can be very effective in overcoming the problems involved.

In many cases of overweight, food is a substitute for affection. The mother who gives her offspring food instead of the love they need is symbolizing her rejection of them because she dares not face the true reason. The greater her unconscious feeling of guilt in connection with this rejection, the better is the table she sets and the more eagerly she urges food upon her children.

The child also senses the rejection, and, craving security, satisfies the craving with over-abundance of food. The desire for food becomes intimately associated with the most profound emotional needs of the individual, and so the pattern is set.

Where a person does not begin to gain weight until later in life, it is well to investigate the immediate emotional background. A wife who feels unsure of her husband's love frequently satisfies that spiritual emptiness with food. A husband whose wife does not satisfy his emotional needs, sexual or otherwise, may compensate by overeating.

The foregoing brief outline indicates the direction that re-education should take.

The average overweight person is not qualified to select

a reducing diet. This should be carefully worked out by the doctor. The word-for-word hypnotic technique that follows will usually insure that the diet is adhered to, and the technique for a daily walk is equally effective. People who weigh too much tend to over-exercise when they get the impulse to reduce.

As soon as the weight has been brought down to the desired level, it might be well to arouse the subject's interest in some form of play or hobby. This applies particularly to people who have been overweight from childhood. Naturally, the patient's own desires and feelings should be consulted.

FOR THE DOCTOR

Hypnotize the patient to medium trance or deeper.

You desire to become strong and slender. You are dissatisfied with yourself as you are. You want to become slender. Because you want to become slender, your appetite is now easily satisfied with a small quantity of food. Your body needs proteins for strength, so you enjoy eating a small quantity of lean meat. You enjoy a single slice of dark, coarse bread. You enjoy eating green leafy vegetables. You enjoy eating all the body-building foods which give you strength, and a proper balance of minerals and vitamims.

Your body already has in storage an abundance of fat. Your body has no need for additional fat. Your body is ready to use this fat that you have stored up. As this fat is used, you look the way you want to look. As this fat is used, you feel the way you want to feel: strong, energetic, vigorous. Because your body has no need for fat now, you have no appetite for fats, sweets, and starches. Because you wish to be slender and strong, you temporarily dislike fats, sweets, and starches. You dislike the fat in meat. You dislike butter. You dislike cream. You dislike ice cream. You dislike candy. You dislike pie. You dislike cake. You dislike potatoes. You dislike white bread.

(Emphasize the dislikes by repeating them)

Your dislike for these foods is becoming so great that it is impossible for you to eat them. You dislike these foods intensely. You dislike them so much that if you tried to force yourself to eat them, you would become nauseated. Your body has no need for these foods right now. Your tastes correspond to the real needs of your body. Food substances that are not needed are actually nauseating to you. If you tried to force yourself to eat a piece of candy, you would become ill and nauseated.

You are finding a new pleasure in eating the foods that your body needs. You eat slowly. You take small bites. You relish each bite as you chew it. You take time to actually taste the flavor of the foods that you eat. You are rediscovering the subtle and enjoyable differences between foods. You enjoy the taste of the lean meat, and a very small quantity of it makes you feel full, satisfied, satisfied. You enjoy the taste of the leafy vegetables. You enjoy the taste of cheese. You enjoy the taste of skimmed milk, which brings you so many valuable minerals. You enjoy the taste of fresh fruits. You enjoy the taste of colored vegetables. You enjoy all of these things so much that a very small quantity of them makes you feel as though you had eaten a Thanksgiving dinner. You are completely satisfied with a quantity of food that contains about *(your advice)* calories.

At this point a specific diet may be read to the patient The kinds and quantities of food for each meal can be specifically stated. The objectives of this diet can also be stated, as follows:

You now weigh (————) pounds. You wish to weigh (so many pounds) because you will feel very much better and be much more attractive. You are going to consume the

138

excess fat from your body at the rate of one pound a week. In (——) weeks you are going to weigh (——) pounds. Each week you consume one pound of your own fatty tissue. You do this because you want to be more attractive. You do this because you want to feel stronger and more vigorous. You do this because you want to be healthy. You do this because you want to be well. You desire to be strong, vigorous, and healthy. That desire is so great that it easily and unconsciously controls your appetite, and you automatically eat only the foods that your body needs, in the quantities that your body requires.

Specific suggestions for reducing certain parts of the body have sometimes proved quite effective, especially when combined with suggestions for exercise which tend to bring these parts of the body to normal. The usual procedure is first to suggest changes in the appetite, and control of the food intake. When this control has been established and the patient is actually eating a smaller quantity of the indicated types of food, suggestions of the following type may be used.

REDUCING ABDOMEN AND HIPS

You are now eating the foods that your body needs. You are eating only the foods that your body needs. You are eating only (——) calories a day, and you are enjoying every bite that you take. In your daily activities you are consuming the reserves of fat that have been stored in your body. This fat is being consumed from the entire body, but it is coming especially from the abdomen and the hips. Your hips are becoming smaller as the fat is consumed. Your abdomen is becoming flat as the fat is consumed. You are feeling stronger and more healthy. You are looking much more attractive. Your hips are becoming smaller. Your abdomen is becoming flatter. Soon your figure will be much better. Soon your figure will be suited to your height and bony structure.

139

DAILY WALK

(Time) may be used to set up a rigid or semi-rigid schedule. Insert "before breakfast," "at 10 o'clock," "after shopping," "two hours after dinner," "before retiring," etc.

Every day at (TIME) you feel restless. Every day at (TIME) you feel the urge to DO something. Every day at (TIME) you have the feeling that you MUST engage in some activity. You have the urge to leave the house and get out in the open air. You feel so good when you get out. You breathe deeply. You breathe from the diaphragm. You begin to walk briskly. You find that it's fun to walk. You feel so good when you start walking. You find yourself stretching. Your body automatically becomes very erect and limber. You feel as though you were supported from above with your body moving lightly and your feet barely touching the ground. You stride freely and easily. Every step that you take makes you feel more vigorous. Every step that you take makes you enjoy even more the sense of well-being throughout your body. You breathe deeply and enjoy the freshness of the air. You enjoy the briskness of your movements. You enjoy the sheer feeling of being alive. You enjoy your movements in the same way that a colt enjoys running across the pasture. You feel alive. You walk in this way for *(distance)*. You enjoy every step of this *(distance)* walk. When you have completed *(distance)* it is with a faint sense of regret that you realize your walk is over. Perhaps next week you will walk a little farther, so that you may have more enjoyment. When your walk is over, you feel completely refreshed, emotionally serene, calm and self-confident, mentally alert and ready to do whatever comes next. Every day your joy in the strength and coordination of your body increases. To move is to be alive, and to be alive is fun. Every day you get more fun out of life. Every day is better than the day before.

140

CHAPTER XVII

BREAKING THE HABIT OF SMOKING

SMOKING NOT THE SAME AS DRINKING

Many authors discuss drinking and smoking as if they are similar behavior patterns. Actually, these two "bad" habits are vastly dissimilar in nature. Excessive drinking affords the drinker a method of escape from the harshness of reality. It is destructive to the tissues of the body. It is, to say the least, an economic and social handicap.

Smoking, on the other hand, is a social ceremony. The habitual gesture of offering your friend a cigarette is an offer of good fellowship. Once the individual has become accustomed to the unusual stimulus of tobacco, it is a pleasant sensaton. It stimulates both taste and smell, tickles the throat pleasantly, and to some degree affects the whole body. It also gives one "something to do with the hands." Its appeal is widespread. However, it is "messy," to some extent costly or at least not essential, and it can be most inconvenient when the habitual smoker finds himself without the "makings" far out in the country, or in the wee small hours of the morning.

MEDICAL REASONS FOR STOPPING SMOKING

The physician will occasionally find it necessary to ask a patient not to smoke, so that some physiological condition can be alleviated or corrected. In using hypnosis under such circumstances to break the habit, it is necessary first to persuade the patient to cooperate. That is, he should be willing to take, first, step one; and then, if necessary, step two of the technique that follows.

METHODS OF USING
HYPNOSIS TO STOP SMOKING

The traditional method of using hypnotic suggestion to stop smoking is to suggest that "it tastes horrible." This suggestion can be effective, but it leaves the person with the craving. It merely takes away the ability to satisfy the craving. The two techniques that follow have been used with excellent effect. The first suggestion is to be used as often as is necessary, that is, until the patient has actually reduced himself to one smoke a day. In many cases it may be deemed advisable by both physician and patient to stop at this point. However, if the smoking habit pattern has to be broken completely, whether from personal wish or by the advice of the physician, the second suggestion should also be used.

Discuss smoking in the waking state. If the patient wishes to stop smoking, and has voluntarily requested that the habit be broken, ask him why. Develop these reasons fully. They can be used later as "feed-back." The therapist has a different problem with the patient who is stopping because of the advice of his physician, and not because of any particular desire of his own. Here it is advisable to establish conscious desire to quit in order to preserve or increase his health, PROVIDED it can be done easily and without effort or longing on his part. The subject is not ready for the hypnotic suggestion until he has a-chieved a state of mind where he WANTS to quit smoking, and says so.

Hypnotize the subject to medium trance level or deeper.

Deeper and deeper to sleep. Deeper and deeper to sleep. You have said that you want to quit smoking. You have said you would like to quit smoking. It is possible for you to do this because we are going to help you to gain a new pleasure from life which will more than replace the pleasure you now get from smoking. Our first step is to enable you to get more pleasure out of smoking.

When a person smokes as much as you do, his taste buds are constantly at work. They become tired. They become insensitive. Right now you cannot taste the very exquisite flavors of either the food you eat or the tobacco you smoke because of the constant stimulation of your taste buds. Your sense of taste might be compared to a man who has been working too hard. He's always tired. We're going to give your taster a rest. Here is the way we are going to do it.

The next time you smoke, your taste buds are going to be especially sensitive. They are going to be so sensitive that you will get a great deal more enjoyment out of smoking than you ever got before. Your enjoyment is going to be so great and you are going to be so well satisfied by this smoking that you will feel no need to smoke again for quite a while. You'll find that you'll want to wait much longer than you would usually wait.

You know how it is when you eat a Thanksgiving dinner. You don't eat turkey very often, so when you do it's a treat. Most people get a great deal of satisfaction from a Thanksgiving dinner. When we finish it we are so well satisfied that for a time food loses all its appeal. We are full. We want no food for a long time. In the same way, when you have finished a smoke which you have thoroughly enjoyed, you are gratified, you are satisfied, you are satiated. You want no more smoking for a long time. That is when the taste buds get a rest. That is when you have a chance to become more sensitive, so that the next time you smoke it is even more satisfying, much more satisfying than the last time. That makes you wait even longer for the next smoke. Each time you smoke it tastes better, as

143

your taste buds become more fresh and clean and responsive. Each time you finish smoking, you are so well satisfied that the rest period between smokes becomes even longer. By tomorrow you will be smoking much less frequently than you smoke today. But the enjoyment of each smoke is so much greater that your total enjoyment is even greater.

Your enjoyment in the things you taste increases daily. Your smoking is more enjoyable. Your food tastes better, much better, very much better. You find that you are enjoying the taste of food more than you have since childhood. Your taste buds are getting a rest, so they are becoming sensitive and more discriminating. The subtle flavors that you used to miss are now a source of great pleasure to you. You eat slowly, tasting each mouthful carefully and getting the utmost pleasure from the taste. Your pleasure in eating, in the tasting of food, in the satisfaction you get from food becomes greater as you smoke less. Each day you smoke less. Each day you smoke less. Soon, you will be smoking only once a day. Soon, you smoke only once a day, and that one smoke is going to give you more pleasure than all the smoking that you now do. Each day you smoke less with more pleasure. Soon you are going to be smoking only once a day. Soon you smoke only once a day.

When the patient has actually reduced his smoking to once a day, if he wishes to eliminate it entirely, we wipe out the habit by transferring the pleasure of this one smoke to the pleasure of eating. This does not necessarily mean an increase in the caloric intake. If the patient needs also to reduce, this suggestion can be combined with suggestions for appetite control as given in the section on reducing. If the patient has no need to control the diet for other purposes, but shows a tendency to eat more than is necessary because of the increased pleasure sense, the situation can be handled with the following suggestion:

Now that you are getting so much pleasure from the food that you eat, you find that the enjoyment is intense with the first few bites that you take. The enjoyment continues to a high level until you have eaten the amount that your body actually needs. When you have eaten the amount that your body needs, the enjoyment ceases. To eat more than that would be just plain hard work. Your enjoyment comes in the quality of food that you eat, and not in the quantity.

To eliminate the final cigarette, get a conscious waking expression of desire from the patient. If he will not say that he wants to quit that one, it is usually futile to make the attempt. If he is undecided, help him to weigh the advantages and disadvantages and come to a decision, but the decision must be his. Follow this with an induction to the medium trance level or deeper.

Deeper and deeper to sleep. Now that you are smoking once a day, you say that you want to stop altogether. You want to eliminate that one smoke, and be a non-smoker. If that is right, nod your head.

Wait.

Very well, we are going to transfer the pleasure you have been getting from this one smoke to two other places. From now on, you get an increased pleasure in eating the first meal of the day. This pleasure is far greater than the pleasure you have been getting from your one smoke. The first bite of food that you take each day tastes so good to you that you get more satisfaction and more gratification than you ever got in smoking. You enjoy all the food that you eat. You particularly enjoy the foods that are most needed by your body. You get an especial gratification from the first food that you eat each day.

You are also going to gain a new gratification in the sense of smell. In eliminating this last smoke, you gain a re-doubled pleasure in smelling the odors of flowers, and the

145

odors of food, and the odors of perfume. The gratification that you used to obtain from tasting and smelling and inhaling tobacco is now more than doubled in your new, keener appreciation of the things that you smell and the food that you taste.

The pleasure of smoking has been transferred into these new pleasures, and smoking can now give you no pleasure at all. For you, tobacco has no taste. For you, tobacco has no taste. For you tobacco has no smell unless someone else is smoking. Your new, keener sense of smell enables you to get a great deal of enjoyment from the smell of tobacco which is being smoked by someone else. If you yourself attempt to smoke, you find no taste and no smell, no taste and no smell, no taste and no smell, no satisfaction of any kind, nothing.

CHAPTER XVIII

HYPNOTIC ANAESTHESIA

ANAESTHESIA AND HYPERAESTHESIA

Condition patient to respond easily to medium trance depth. Hypnotize as deeply as possible.

Let us imagine that you are standing in front of a gas stove (or electric or wood stove). On a table to the left of the stove is a pail of icy salt water. Standing on the stove itself, and to your right, is a pail of warm water. You can see these pails in front of you. As soon as you see them, nod your head. *(Wait for nod.)* All right, you see them clearly now.

Dip your left hand into the pail of icy water. Plunge it to the bottom. As you probably know, salt water can become colder than unsalted water before freezing, and so the water into which you have put your hand is actually *below* the normal freezing point of water, so far as temperature is concerned. It is below 32 degrees Fahrenheit. It is colder than zero Centigrade.

Your hand is now extended to the bottom of this pail of extremely cold water. At first, your hand feels very cold, but then it begins to get numb, numb and insensitive, numb and unfeeling. Just leave your hand there as it continues to get more and more numb. Soon it will be so numb that if we had to cut it with a knife you would not feel it. Perhaps you would feel a slight pushing sensation, as though we were pushing at your hand through a heavy leather glove, but

147

that would be all. There is a good possibility that you would feel nothing at all, nothing at all.

Now, while your left hand continues to get more and more numb, plunge your right hand into the warm water.

As you do so, you begin immediately to feel the warmth creeping through your flesh. Now, I'm going to turn the heat on under the pail of warm water and make the water hotter.

While I do this, the icy water remains colder than ice, and your left hand becomes completely numb and insensitive to all feeling.

Now, the heat is on under the pail of warm water, and the water is slowly getting hotter. As it gets hotter and hotter, your hand is going to become very sensitive. You have had a burn at some time in your life, haven't you? *(Wait for nod.)* The burned spot was very sensitive to the touch, wasn't it? *(Wait)* As the water gets hotter, your hand is going to get very sensitive. The skin is already becoming red and raw. It is becoming red and raw. Your hand is becoming more and more sensitive. As the water gets hotter, your hand is going to get very sensitive. As the water gets hotter and hotter, the skin of your hand becomes more and more red, more and more sensitive. As the water continues to get hotter, it will soon reach the point where you can no longer stand it.

When you can no longer stand it, say "Ouch!" right out loud, and pull both of your hands out of the pails. As soon as you can no longer stand the heat, say "Ouch!" and pull both of your hands out of the pails. If you understand me clearly, please nod your head.

Wait for the subject to react. If after five minutes there is no reaction, ask the subject to take his hands out of the pails, and proceed with the tests.

Now your hands feel very different. Your left hand is

cold and numb. It is completely insensitive and without feeling. Your right hand is very sensitive, painfully sensitive, so sensitive that the slightest touch would feel as though I had driven a nail right through your hand. I have here a sterilized needle. I am going to touch your right hand with that needle, and it will feel as though I were driving a spike right through your hand.

Touch right hand with needle point. Observe flinch and withdrawal. If there is no reaction, ask if it seemed sensitive. Make sure that no matter how little the difference, the subject realizes that there was a difference in the feeling. It may in some cases be necessary to wait until you have also tested the anaesthetized hand in order to insure that the subject is aware of the difference.

Now I am going to touch the left hand with the same sterilized needle. Your left hand is very numb and insensitive. You may feel a slight push as though you were wearing a heavy leather glove.

Prick the left hand with the needle. First test the insensitive areas on the back of the hand.

You see, your hand is numb. Your hand is numb and insensitive. How does it feel? Tell me how it feels.

Wait for the subject's description. If it proves necessary to reinforce this conditioning, or in future anaesthesias, when you wish to induce them rapidly, use the "feedback method." Use the subject's own words as a basis for further suggestions.

That's right. It feels numb and insensitive. Now, we are going to test the ball of the thumb, the part that is usually very sensitive. Your whole hand is cold and numb. The ball of the thumb is especially numb.

Test deeply.

Do you see the difference? Do you feel a distinct difference between your right and left hands? *(Wait)* Of course you do. Now, we are going to awaken you. Your left hand is going to remain numb and insensitive even after you awaken. Your right hand is going to remain raw and sensitive, very sensitive, even after you awaken. Wake up now with your hands still feeling the same. Wake up, one, two, three. WIDE AWAKE.

Test the response while the subject is watching. In many cases there will be no change in the response. The post-hypnotic anaesthesia will be as effective as the hypnotic anaesthesia. In other cases there will be a lessening of the effect but still a noticeable difference. In some cases the visual stimulus of seeing the needle enter the skin will produce sufficient auto-suggestion to overcome the effect of the hypnotic suggestion. In such cases, ask the subject to close his or her eyes. This may be sufficient to re-establish the anaesthesia and the hyperaesthesia. After the subject is satisfied that a difference of feeling exists between the two hands, both in hypnosis and in the waking state, re-hypnotize him with the accustomed technique.

Now, your hands are becoming normal. Your right hand feels cool and comfortable, cool and comfortable, perfectly normal. Your left hand is becoming warm and comfortable, warm and comfortable. Visualize the pails again. See the pails again. Dip your left hand in the warm pail, and take it out feeling perfectly normal. Dip your right hand in the icy water, and take it out feeling perfectly normal. Both hands are now normal in every way, completely normal, normal in every way.

You're beginning to wake up now. At the count of three you'll be wide awake, and completely normal, your hands perfectly normal. Wake up, one, two, three. WIDE AWAKE.

CHAPTER XIX

PAINLESS CHILDBIRTH

By definition, painless childbirth occurs when the mother who is bearing the child goes through the process without experiencing physical pain.

CONDITION DEFINITELY ANAESTHETIC

The validity of hypnotic anaesthesia has been debated. Theories have been advanced that there is no true anaesthesia, but merely amnesia for the hurt that was experienced. Much reliable testimony and experience has disproved these theories, and established hypnotic anaesthesia as a fact.

Amnesia for the experience is not only unnecessary but is actually undesirable. The patient who is responsive to a depth adequate for amnesia need experience no pain whatsoever, provided her training is adequate.

WIDESPREAD FEAR OF CHILDBIRTH

Childbirth, a natural and almost universal physiological function of the female human, has come to be regarded with fear and apprehension, sometimes with downright terror, by modern American and Western European women. Women have been taught to expect pain and to fear childbirth from early girlhood.

SIMPLE EDUCATION VALUABLE

By an intensive education—without hypnosis—concerning the structure and function of the female body, it is possible to lay an effective framework of confidence and anticipation for the coming labor. Grantly Dick Read[29] reports outstanding results with such an approach to the problem. His hypothesis is that the pain which has been, and still is, experienced by the vast majority of women during labor and delivery, is the product of fear. As he reports it, women who have been adequately prepared, bear their children not only without "pain," but actually in many cases with a sense of exultation.

It should be noted that Read's method of education does not include hypnosis.

HYPNOSIS A POWERFUL AID TO
PAINLESS CHILDBIRTH

Because it directly affects the "unconscious" mind, hypnosis has proved to be a catalyst in the education and re-education of the woman who expects a child. The nine-month period between conception and delivery offers ample opportunity for a program of re-education and suggestion. The effectiveness of hypnosis, where it can be induced, can greatly reduce the time needed for the necessary work.

The necessary hypnotic conditioning can be completed fairly early in the pregnancy. The balance of the time may then be divided between brief reinforcement of the conditioning along with the educational details as described by Read. Some sex education may be necessary. Many superstitions and fears must be removed. By this combination of hypnosis with education and suggestion, the expectant mother is trained to approach her experience with courage and anticipation, with a knowledge based on past experience that hypnotic anaesthesia is a fact *for her*, and that childbirth is a normal, natural, physiological function of her body.

CONDITIONING FOR PAINLESS CHILDBIRTH
A STEP BY STEP PROCESS

The training involved should follow an orderly pattern of conditioning. The first step is to induce a hypnotic response. Then the response should be speeded up until the patient is able to achieve medium or deep trance in a few seconds at a given signal.

She must next be conditioned in a localized anaesthesia. When this has been satisfactorily achieved, the fourth step is instantaneous anaesthesia in response to a signal. This is accomplished while the subject is in hypnosis.

The fifth step is conditioning her to achieve post-hypnotic anaesthesia. And finally, the sixth step is the establishment of anaesthetic response to a signal given while the patient is in the waking state.

This completes the preliminary hypnotic conditioning. The responses should be reinforced from time to time.

SIGNAL RESPONSE

There is no fixed signal response. The physical act of entering the hospital doors is a useful standard signal for the establishment of anaesthesia. Physicians who have used the recognition of "labor contractions" as a signal for the establishment of anaesthesia report that patients frequently delay reporting at the hospital until they are completely dilated. Whatever the signal, it is impressed in somewhat the following manner:

The patient, having been conditioned in anaesthesia, *knows* that it is possible for her to be tested for pain without experiencing pain. Her knowledge is based upon her own past experience with hypnotic anaesthesia. By extrapolation, she is going to go through this other PERFECTLY NATURAL AND NORMAL physiological experience in comfort and composure. She is going to know what is going on. She is going to be alert and is going to participate fully in the experience. She is fully able to cooperate with the doctor and to respond to his suggestions at all times. She is going to be alert and able to hear and enjoy her baby's first cry.

This training, like the conditioning in hypnosis and anaesthesia, can be completed fairly early in the pregnancy.

IMPORTANCE OF REINFORCING SUGGESTIONS

It is not to be expected that one simple suggestion on the part of the physician or hypnotist can always overcome the force of early training in fear and expectation of pain. It does happen occasionally, but even with a good subject it is better to reinforce the suggestion many times.

The value of the educational procedures herein outlined lies in the fact that sudden switch of physicians or hospitals would not invalidate the conditioning. The patient has learned a self-discipline and self-control which is not necessarily keyed in with the personality of the physician.

ONLY DANGER LIES IN
A NEGATIVE ENVIRONMENT

Nurses, orderlies and other physicians are, unfortunately, steeped in the old beliefs as deeply as was formerly the patient herself. Careless talk can decrease the effect of even the best of conditionings. Such questions as "How are the *pains* now?" could in some cases re-establish a part of the old fear.

Efforts should be made to eliminate the possibility of such a negative environment. This would require the cooperation of orderlies, nurses, etc. The ideal situation is one in which EVERY person who comes in contact with the patient takes the positive attitude, and uses such phrases as labor CONTRACTIONS, muscle CONTRACTIONS, and aids the conditioning and educational work of the doctor in both speech and conduct.

154

The doctor must also school himself. He must eliminate the words "labor pains" from his vocabulary.

After a few successful experiences with painless delivery, the doctor will develop a confidence in the effectiveness of this conditioning, which will be reflected in his manner.

SUGGESTIONS FOR
NATURAL (PAINLESS) CHILDBIRTH

Pre-condition the expectant mother in hypnosis and an-aesthesia as detailed in previous pages. Hypnotize, test for anaesthesia, and proceed.

You are going to bear a child. The child is now within you, developing, growing, preparing for entry into the world. You look forward to this time. Your child's birth is going to be a completely natural event in your life. Among primitive peoples the arrival of a child is a joyful experience for the mother. Childbirth is joyful because the mother is unafraid. She has *never* been taught to fear this perfectly natural process of her body. Because she is courageous, her muscles are relaxed. When the long muscles of the womb contract to expel the baby from her body, the round muscles which have held the baby safely in her body relax. The natural process of moving a baby out of the mother's body is accomplished as easily and as peacefully as eating or breathing, or digesting food, or moving the bowels, or any other natural process of the body. A healthy, courageous mother gives birth to a healthy baby with joy and relaxation. The process is natural, effortless, automatic. You are courageous, you are relaxed, you know that you, also, have the ability to deliver your child in peace and relaxation. The act of bearing your child will be as natural and easy as the other processes of your body. You are courageous. You are relaxed. You know that the birth of your child will be a joyful event in your life. You are courageous. You are re-

155

laxed. Your muscles work together. When the long muscles contract to move the baby out of your body, the round muscles relax. The more the long muscles contract, the more the round muscles relax. The sets of muscles in your body work together. The rest of your body is relaxed and peaceful. You are joyful. You will be alert to hear your baby's first cry. You are relaxed and peaceful. You are courageous. You are relaxed and peaceful. You are brave. You are composed. You are confident.

CHAPTER XX

HYPNOSIS IN DENTISTRY

The use of suggestion and hypnosis in some form by every dentist is not only possible but, as the dentist reader will realize as he reads the following, it can become a vital part of his day to day practice.

Suggestion and hypnosis need not take up extra time. A number of techniques have been worked out for the dentist so that he can make use of the power of words and of his own office equipment in a way that he has perhaps never considered possible.

Today, the science of dentistry has made available methods of chemical anaesthesia which make dentistry a painless and relaxed procedure for the patient—if only the dentist can persuade the patient that such is indeed the case. Unfortunately, many and perhaps even most of his patients react in terms of other people's experiences and fears, and their own past experience. A good percentage of these traumatic experiences occurred before the development of modern painless techniques. And the fearful attitude which the average person brings into the dentist's office is often an attitude that has been communicated to him by someone else.

The dentist, unlike the medical doctor, the psychologist, the psychoanalyst or the psychiatrist, is not usually concerned with the deeper problems of emotional adjustment. But he is very much concerned with the patient's emotional attitudes toward dentistry and the dental situation. In order to solve this important problem successfully, he should be in a position to help the patient overcome aglophobia (fear of pain). If we may coin a phrase, he must help the patient overcome "dentiphobia."

"Dentiphobia" is an anxiety state with acute reactions at the first sign of activity on the part of the dentist. It is frequently encountered with patients who have a surface control of their behavior while in the dentist chair. This takes the form of muscular rigidity and tension. It is also expressed with dizzy and fainting spells.

USE IN DENTISTRY OF HYPNOTIC ANAESTHESIA IS LIMITED

The dentist who has heard of the use of hypnosis in connection with his work frequently has the impression that hypnosis provides a means of inducing anaesthesia without chemical means. It can be used, of course, for such a purpose, and certainly it is worth knowing the techniques involved. A dentist who is a skillful hypnotist can use an undisguised hypnotic technique (that is, one in which the patient has given his consent to the use of hypnosis) and produce an anaesthesia which would be quite satisfactory for oral surgery.

He could induce such an anaesthesia quickly in approximately one-fifth of his patients. With a longer period of training, an additional three-fifths of his patients could be anaesthetized. The remaining one-fifth would require much too long a training period for the practical use of hypnosis.

Few dentists, however, would find it economically possible to devote the time necessary to induce these responses. Futhermore, the dentist who uses hypnosis openly in his practice today faces the task of re-educating his patients and overcoming many misconceptions regarding the hypnotic situation. It is for that reason that hypnotism is today only occasionally used openly in dental practice.

The important exception to this general rule is the patient who cannot be given a chemical anaesthetic for one reason or another. These reasons include heart condition, allergic reactions, and general physical health. Under such conditions, an open technique may be indicated, and the patient may be willing to spend the time necessary for conditioning in hypnotic response. If the dentist is unable to devote the time to condition the patient he may call upon a medical or psychological specialist for conditioning.

THE USE OF PENTATHOL SODIUM
AS A HYPNOTIC AGENT

There is a surprise in store for many dentists who use pentathol sodium for anaesthetic purposes. Although the patient may appear to be unconscious when pentathol sodium has been used, actually he is in a chemically induced trance. In this state he will react to suggestions in much the same manner as a person who has been hypnotized to deep trance in the ordinary fashion.

Rather than go into a detailed narrative account here of what can be done in this type of trance, the authors offer the following experience of a dentist trained by one of the authors. This dentist had, of course, learned the possibilities of controlling hemorrhages by hypnotic suggestion, and he had learned to give powerful suggestions for well-being that would carry over after the patient was awakened. With this training behind him, he determined to test the reactions of a patient having an extraction while anaesthetized with pentathol sodium.

After performing the extraction, he suggested vigorously to the woman that the bleeding would stop. It did stop. He realized that the reaction might have been a coincidence and that one test could not prove a rule. He tried a few more suggestions. Instead of wheeling the patient into the recovery room, he gave her vigorous suggestions that she would be able to walk the distance easily. She did so. He then suggested with equal vigor the usual "super-wonderful" awakening which is part of the hypnotic pattern, and left her.

As the doctor phrased it later in describing what happened, "You know how they are. You help them on with their shoes, put their hats on their heads, put their purses in their hands, and steer them out to a taxi. They really are foggy."

But now the situation was different. After a reasonable time the dentist re-entered the recovery room to check on his patient. Here is how he described the condition in which he found her.

"She was all ready to go home. She had her shoes and hat on. Most significant of all, she had repaired her make-up. She *was* wide-awake, and seemed to be doing nicely. The post-hypnotic suggestion for anaesthesia must have had its effect also. For she said her mouth felt fine."

NEGATIVE DENTAL TECHNIQUES
CAN BE CHANGED

The tradition of pain and discomfort in dentistry has become well established. A great many dentists are continuously on the defensive. Lacking a knowledge of the positive approach, they say, "This won't hurt!" Or worse, they warn, "Now, this will hurt a little." Many have fallen into the habit of negative thinking to such an extent that they use the negative approach as part of their attitude. "Now, this won't be uncomfortable." "Now, you're not going to feel any pain, so don't worry." "This is going to cost a lot, I'm afraid, but it will really be worth it."

The dentist who follows these verbal patterns should give himself a searching examination. He has been taken in by

160

the same propaganda that has affected his patients. He also believes that dental operations are painful, and he seems to have a compulsion to feel apologetic about it.

His first job, therefore, is to convince himself that the practice of dentistry is not merely a means of making a living. Actually, when he begins to investigate this aspect of his work, he finds it easy to establish a sound emotional basis for both pride and a sense of service to humanity. The dentist's job is no sinecure. It requires skill and hard work. It must have behind it a background of training and knowledge. Its aim is to provide relief from discomfort and even agony, and in no case is the dentist himself responsible for the original ache or pain that brings patients into his office. As a group, and as individuals, dentists can number themselves among the comparatively few who have deliberately trained themselves to bring relief and surcease for the trials and tribulations of the many.

The dentist's second task in connection with his own attitude is to learn to believe that the anaesthetic agents he uses *are* effective, and that any normal patient can be very comfortable in the dental chair. The first step in this process is to eliminate consciously from his vocabulary the words 'pain," "hurt," "uncomfortable," "discomfort," etc. As his knowledge of the profound effect of suggestion develops, the dentist will find himself using the right words automatically. And, of course, he should train his nurses and assistants to use positive suggestion with the patients. It is important to avoid "loose talk" and negative suggestions which might be picked up by the patient. Negative words in relation to dentistry should *never* be uttered by anyone in a dental office.

Since this point cannot be over-stated, the following illustration is offered as an example of what can happen. A woman who had been referred to a psychologist as a "migraine headache case" was taught autohypnosis and autohypnotic anaesthesia as an aid to the process of psychotherapy. Some time after her therapy was successfully terminated she went to her dentist to have a tooth filled. She hypnotized herself as soon as she had seated herself in the chair, and suggested an oral anaesthesia, which was profound. The dentist was unaware of what she had done. He merely thought she was a "good patient."

She naturally remained "cooperative," so that she could comply with the dentist's requests. Although she did not realize it, she was responding to his suggestions. He worked for some time and she enjoyed perfect comfort. He then suddenly warned her, "Now, this is going to hurt." And immediately proceeded to do what was necessary. It did hurt. It hurt like fury. It hurt as only a pain intensified tenfold by hypnosis can hurt. It would have been just as easy for her to respond to a positive suggestion, but instead she responded to a negative suggestion which was probably uttered quite automatically by the dentist.

Had the dentist said, "Now, I'm going to work a little closer (or a little harder, or a little deeper); you just relax, and you'll be perfectly comfortable; the deeper I work, the more you'll relax, and you'll feel comfortable," she would have felt nothing beyond her previous experience.

POSITIVE APPROACH HAS
MANY ASPECTS

Very few dentists make proper psychological capital out of their well-engineered equipment. The dental chair of today is a versatile instrument. It can be adjusted to fit almost any human body. It is capable of giving the body maximum support with a minimum of muscular tension. A few minutes spent in pointing this out to the patient while the dentist is doing necessary preliminary work will pay dividends. The chair should be adjusted with consideration for both the comfort of the patient and the convenience of the dentist. The dentist can remark that many of his patients go to sleep while he is working on them. This suggestion should be used with every new patient, and persisted in until it becomes a normal part of the dentist's conversation. The results will be surprising.

The concept that the dental office can be a place for relaxation is new. The patient will think about it. He will begin to relax. If such a preliminary approach is followed with a few direct suggestions for relaxation, a large percentage will "let go." This makes the work much easier for both dentist and patient.

A dentist who has studied the verbal patterns that make up positive suggestion technique, and who has learned how hypnosis works, will find many opportunities in the course of a day to use his knowledge. A pedodontist recently reported that after mastering these techniques he "mixed equal parts of novocaine and suggestion" with remarkable results.

There is nothing unusual in obtaining good results in working with children. This particular dentist's patients range from children three years old to young people of fifteen. With the three-year olds he uses a direct approach without any preliminary suggestions of a trance-inducing nature. This approach is justified because a very young child has a comparatively high development of the mental processes of identification and a comparatively low development of discrimination. Such a child can be treated as though he were *always hypnotized.*

With older children the best method is to combine a fixation technique or a relaxing technique with suggestion. The result will usually be equally effective.

DENTAL COSTS JUSTIFIABLE

A dentist who has learned to control his own attitudes and the attitudes of his patients in the direction of greater comfort will soon find that he has a new outlook on his work. He will no longer feel so apologetic about the necessarily high expense of extensive dental repair.

The dentists of America are doing a tremendous job in their attempt to educate the public. The emphasis on preventive dentistry is a tribute to the profession. Every dentist should be proud of his profession and the humanitarian work he is doing. His attitudes toward the patient should reflect this pride, and it should also show clearly that he has confidence in his own skill and in his ability to help his patient in comfort and relaxation.

To achieve such an important purpose, a knowledge of the techniques of hypnosis and suggestion are virtually indispensible.

DENTAL ANAESTHESIA

In the following technique, hypnosis is openly used. The patient should be hypnotized to the medium trance level if possible, and conditioned for the anaesthesia. Before attempting anaesthesia, explore the patient's previous experience in regard to chemical anaesthesia. If the patient has previously and satisfactorily experienced a novocaine anaesthesia, the suggestion may run as follows. (Note: Where the word "area" is used, substitute "Right side of lower jaw," "left side of upper jaw," "whole mouth," etc.)

Now the (area) is going to feel just as though we had given you a big injection of a strong solution of novocaine. Soon you will begin to feel it take effect. Soon you will begin to feel the numb, tingling sensation in your (area). Just as soon as you begin to feel the tingling and numbness, lift your right (or left) hand two or three inches. The (area) is becoming more and more numb, more and more numb, more and more numb. As soon as you feel the tingling and numbness raise your hand two or three inches. *(Wait)*

The doctor may at this time leave the patient and do other

164

necessary things, he may silently observe the patient, or he may continue softly saying, "More and more numb, more and more numb, etc.," until *the patient acknowledges some difference in feeling by raising the hand.*

All right, drop your hand, and let it relax completely. Now the (area) is becoming more and more numb, more and more numb, so numb that you can feel absolutely nothing. Your (area) is becoming so numb that I can do all the work we have to do, and you will feel absolutely nothing. You may at times feel a sort of a push or pressure, but otherwise you can feel absolutely nothing. Open your mouth wide now, and you will see what I mean.

Pierce the gum tissue in a normally sensitive spot. Push the needle in fairly deep, and at the same time say:

You see, it's completely numb. Maybe you feel a push. The harder I push the more numb it gets. Maybe you feel absolutely nothing. On the other hand, when I touch you with a needle over here, it's perfectly normal.

For a control, test lightly on the other side. In both tests, watch carefuly for any signs of flinching. If necessary, you may ask the patient's opinion. REMEMBER, hypnotic anaesthesia is a fact. It is an actual raising of the threshold of pain. It is not that the patient experiences pain but has amnesia for that fact, as has been previously postulated by some psychologists. If the anaesthesia is complete, the patient will feel no pain, although he may be perfectly alert.

Now, keep going deeper and deeper. Go deeper with every breath that you take. Relax more and more, and go deeper with every breath that you take. I am going to go to work now. I am going to do the necessary things to make your mouth healthy, well and strong, so just keep going deeper while I work. The more I work, the more numb it gets. The harder I work (push, pull, drill, etc.) the more the numbness grows.

From here on, the dentist can instruct the patient to co-

165

operate as though he were awake, and a chemical anaesthesia were being used. The patient can spit, etc. Keep emphasizing, "The more I work, the better or number you feel." When the work is done, restore the feeling of normalcy to all except the operated area in the following manner:

Now the work is finished for today, so we are going to bring back most of the feeling. But we are going to leave the feeling blocked off in the spots where I worked. Even when the numbness and tingling has gone, your mouth is going to feel absolutely perfect, extremely comfortable. Now, the normal feeling is beginning to come back into your mouth. The feeling is becoming more and more normal, more and more normal. Soon, your mouth will be completely normal. As soon as it is normal, raise your right hand.

Wait. As soon as the subject feels that the mouth is normal, check with the needle prick. If necessary, reinforce the suggestion for normalcy.

Soon, we are going to awaken you. Even after you are wide awake, and no longer hypnotized, the places where we worked will feel perfectly comfortable and perfectly normal. You are going to walk out of this office feeling marvelous. You are going to leave this office feeling refreshed by the perfect relaxation that you have enjoyed in this chair. You will always find the dental chair a wonderful place to relax. You will always leave the dental office feeling better than when you came in.

Usual awakening technique.

CONTROL OF SALIVA

The salivary glands are strongly influenced by emotions. Their activity is also regulated with comparative ease by hypnotic suggestion. Tell the hypnotized subject on whom you are working:

166

Now, your salivary glands are going to stop working. When you put food in your mouth, the salivary glands automatically start to work, but it's hard for them to tell the difference between my instruments and food. So we will just point out that difference to them. It is better for you if your mouth becomes dry right now. So your mouth is becoming dry. The salivary glands are no longer working. Your mouth is no longer becoming moist. Your mouth is becoming dry. Your mouth is becoming dry, and it is going to stay dry for as long as I am working on it. When I stop working, your mouth will become normally moist, but as long as I am working on you, your mouth is going to stay dry, very dry.

CONTROL OF HEMORRHAGE

Hypnotic suggestion for the control of hemorrhage after a complicated extraction is frequently effective. The suggestion may be made as follows:

The tooth is out now, and everything is just fine. The blood is flowing freely, washing the socket sweet and clean. The blood is flowing freely and we will let it flow for a little while. When it has flowed long enough, and I tell it to stop, the bleeding will stop. When I tell the bleeding to stop, it will stop.

(Wait until you are ready to stop the flow of blood.)

The bleeding is going to stop now. The bleeding is stopping. The bleeding has stopped. The bleeding has stopped, and there will be no more bleeding. The blood will form a nice healthy clot in the socket, and the cut is going to heal very rapidly. The socket is going to heal very rapidly. The socket is going to heal rapidly, and be perfectly healthy.

CHAPTER XXI

WORKING WITH CHILDREN

WHEN HYPNOTIC RESPONSE CAN BE EXPECTED

The very young child cannot be hypnotized in the conventional sense. Generally speaking, a child under five years old can neither concentrate on nor understand any of the induction techniques used with older children and with adults. Occasionally, a very bright child of four or five, particularly one who has occasion to watch an "open" technique being used on others, can not only learn to be hypnotized, but can also learn the pattern of hypnotizing another individual. Such virtuosity is unimportant in itself except insofar as it emphasizes that, even with children, nothing should be taken for granted.

Children can be hypnotized as soon as they acquire connotations to words. With the development of the functions of the cerebral cortex and with the acquirement of verbal patterns and associations comes a development in critical discrimination. There is no abrupt transition but rather a gradual diminishment of the state of infantile suggestibility and a gradual enlargement of the powers of judgment.

At a period some time between five and eight years old, children become hypnotizable in the conventional sense. Precocious individuals may reach this stage earlier. Retarded mental development may delay or completely prevent the child from attaining the hypnotizable stage.

Most adults are aware that the little child "believes" the simple statements made to it by grown-ups. Tell a child,

"Yes, Virginia, there is a Santa Claus!" At Christmas time, maintain the semblance of the story with a little mystery, and the child will believe that Santa Claus is a real person.

When little Willie falls down and bumps his knee it hurts. He comes running to mother with tears streaming down his face. Mother says, "That's all right, Willie. Mother will kiss it and make it well. It won't hurt any more." She kisses it, and miraculously enough it stops hurting. Willie dries his tears and goes happily back to play. For him, it *doesn't* hurt any more. Mother has induced a hypnotic analgesia.

Parents should always be urged to deal patiently with the aches and pains of little children. The process of making it well should always be completed, even if it seems farcical and childish. It is neither. The great well-spring of faith in mother or father is at work, and it can work wonders.

TECHNIQUES OF HYPNOSIS
FOR VERY YOUNG CHILDREN

The most primitive hypnotic technique has been used by mothers throughout all recorded history. Rocking baby to sleep and singing baby to sleep are two of the most potent hypnotic influences, utilizing as they do monotonous tactile stimulation and monotonous auditory stimulation. Such stimuli work on the child's nervous system in the same way that they would work on the systems of the more highly developed and organized adults. Pavlov tells us that the same type of stimuli are also successful in lulling animals to sleep.

It is important to differentiate between sleep *per se* and hypnosis. The infant who is "always hypnotized" and the animals in the experimental laboratories are lulled from a state of "waking hypnosis" into slumber. As a child develops through the third and fourth years (of normal growth) it is possible to utilize hypnotic techniques in inducing slumber and also for amplifying the effect of very simply worded and direct therapeutic suggestions. For instance, a child that is being lulled into slumber can be told, "Tomorrow, you're going to be so happy. All day long you're going to be so very happy. You like everybody and everybody likes you." It is very difficult to formulate suggestions concerning behavior or emotional patterns which can be understood and accepted by the child at this period. But effective results can be obtained by a repetition of any simple, positive statement involving the child's daily life.

THE HYPNOTIZABLE CHILD

As has been said, most children become hypnotizable between the ages of five and six. Most of them continue to be easily hypnotizable until they reach the age of about fourteen, after which there is a gradual falling off. The percentage of young people of twenty who can be hypnotized easily and deeply the first time is still well above the norm (which is one out of five adults), but apparently the tensions of the struggle of existence have set in. Swiftly, then, the individual develops "conscious" and "unconscious" resistances, and it becomes necessary to use relaxation techniques as a preliminary to, or concurrently with, attention fixation methods.

TECHNIQUES FOR HYPNOTIZING CHILDREN

The emphasis is on simplicity. Obviously, the younger child simply cannot understand most of the high level vocabulary of Chapter II. Repetitive techniques involving one or two easily understandable ideas are extremely effective. The nature of these will vary, of course, depending on the situation and the interpersonal relationship between the hypnotist and the subject. But, generally speaking, the pattern is as follows: "You are going to sleep, you are becoming sleepy, you *are* asleep, and going into a deeper sleep!" Each step in the process should be repeated as often as seems necessary. Anyone who has read the detailed induction technique of Chapter II will know how prolonged such a process can be if conditions are poor. No absolute rule can be given, but children will usually respond very much faster than adults.

Young children love repetitive stories. For this reason, a story-telling technique can be very useful in hypnotizing them. Almost anyone who remembers his own childhood can place Brer Rabbit, Teddy Bear, Sleeping Beauty, or the more recent Mickey Mouse and his cartoon cousins in some kind of a story situation. Ask the child to close his eyes, then appeal to his visual imagination, and so make the story very real. As the child becomes relaxed, as the restless movements stop, the suggestions of sleep can be woven in.

As soon as the eyeballs are observed (through the closed lids) to turn up, or to roll in an uncoordinated manner, an eye catalepsy or other test suggestion can be made.

At all times be aware of the vocabulary level of the child. A misunderstanding may cause him to open his eyes to ask what you said. If this happens, the induction will usually have to be started again at the beginning.

SYMPTOM TREATMENT FOR CHILDREN

A child misbehaves principally for reasons of anxiety. Most of the anti-social acts of children are rooted in fear. A child that wets the bed or cries at night feels insecure. The average parent endures these irritations anticipating that presently the child will outgrow them, and presently the child seems to do so. The symptom of bed wetting, for instance, ceases, and the problem is "solved." On the other hand, any therapist using the following suppressed techniques must do so with the full realization that the suppression of one symptom may cause increased anxiety or may lead to the relief of the anxiety by the development of another symptom. At times it may be advisable to suppress a symptom for social reasons while expressive psychotherapy is used to alter the basic psychological condition of which the bed wetting or nail-biting is merely a symptom.

Generally speaking, it is unnecessary for parents to endure the more unpleasant symptoms of anxiety such as—again—bed wetting. Just as the child learns later to suppress such manifestations itself without affecting the underlying emotional problems, so direct hypnotic suggestion can be used to suppress the symptom as soon as the child reaches the hypnotizable age. Usually, with or without hypnosis in this simple form of treatment, the basic emotional problem remains.

A number of word-for-word techniques are given in Part II of Chapter XXII for bed wetting, nail biting, and other symptoms of anxiety.

PSYCHOTHERAPY FOR CHILDREN

There is an old saw to the effect, "Little children, little problems; big children, big problems." What this means is that the emotionally tangled six-year old grows up to be an even more tangled twelve-year old. The complications, once started, become worse, not better, unless something is done, and done *right*. Sometimes, intentionally or by accident, parents supply the child an environment where he is able to thrive and where, within normal limitations, he grows up free of the serious neurotic tendencies that threatened to overcome him when he was a baby. However, many parents are not good judges of what constitutes a favorable environment for their children. Indeed, some parents, impatient, quick-tempered, intent on making a living, or doing the thousand daily tasks attendant on bringing up a family, are the child's most dangerous emotional problems. It is a problem, moreover, from which he cannot escape. Mother and father are not aware when some brief, quickly forgotten

172

(by them) outburst of fury has caused a trauma in their offspring.

Children simply do not understand that mother's dark mood, product perhaps of financial trouble, or of sickness, is not a direct and personal hatred. Unless such childhood traumas are skillfully offset immediately, or treated later on by a psychotherapist, they "grow up" with the individual, looming ever larger. The "unconscious" seems to have no judgment. Without trained guidance it is incapable of reducing childhood incidents to their proper unimportant perspective in the individual's life. And the saner thoughts of the developing "conscious" mind seem to have no effect on such a shock area.

HYPNOTIC PROCEDURES FOR CHILD PSYCHOTHERAPY

a

When prolonged hypnotherapy is indicated, several problems arise which are special to children. First, there is the hypnotic induction itself. Most chidren can be hypnotized so easily that there is a great temptation on the part of the hypnotist to be satisfied with lighter responses. When this happens, the child may simply display twitchings, squirmings, and restless behavior. Smiling during the induction or at intervals during the trance is observed, and occasionally even the the skilled operator wonders whether the child is hypnotized and responsive, or whether he is merely "cooperating."

In Chapter XXII there is a word-for-word technique that will enable any hypnotist to discover if a child is malingering.

b

Children would rather play than go to a psychologist. By the time the average emotionally tangled child is brought to a psychotherapist, he may have been the "rounds." His distracted parents have done "everything," and taken him "everywhere." Such a child is no longer in awe of the professional man, and in fact has developed a cynical outlook on the medical profession. He is "fed up."

His interest must be aroused and held. All child specialists have this problem to some extent, but for the psychotherapist it is a must. A prolonged therapy involves many visits, and there must be alleviations or the strain on the child will be considerable.

One psychologist works half an hour at a time on a difficult child. The first fifteen minutes he devotes (if the patient is a boy) to taking him, for example:

(1)   On an hallucinatory airplane ride. This theme can be used several times with the planes becoming faster and more powerful.

(2)   On an hallucinary ride to the moon on a rocket ship.

(3)   On a big game hunt in Africa.

(4)   On a swordfish trip off the California coast.

Other stories will suggest themselves as time goes by, and the hypnotherapist will gradually build up a fund of them for all purposes. To some extent, the pleasure of hallucinatory activity, or of simple illusions, offsets for the child the loss of play time, which is frequently felt very keenly by children of all ages.

CHAPTER XXII

WORKING WITH CHILDREN

INDUCTION

Have available a one cent piece and a larger coin. A quarter or a half dollar offers the youngster a great incentive. The child is hypnotized and while in the suspected medium or deep trance is given the following suggestions:

I am putting a penny against your thumb now.

Accompany your words with the action.

Place your forefinger against it. That's right. Now, your finger and thumb are stuck fast to that penny. The penny is stuck tight between your thumb and finger. Your thumb is stuck to the penny. Your finger is stuck to the penny. You can't drop it. You can't throw it away. You can't take it away from your thumb and finger with the other hand. Your other hand will just slip off of it. That penny is stuck to your thumb and forefinger now. Try to throw it away or drop it or take it away. You just can't do it. The penny is stuck to your finger. You can't get rid of it.

Give the subject an opportunity to test the challenge.

You see, it's stuck tight. That penny is going to remain stuck in your hand, even after you wake up. The penny is going to stay stuck until I scratch my head. When I scratch my head you can let go of the penny but not before. When I scratch my head you can let go of the penny.

Awaken the subject with suggestion for complete amnesia. (See Chapter II, Paragraphs 43 and 44.)

"Hello, what have you got in your hand? Why are you holding it so tight? Will you give it to me?"

Subject will usually rationalize and refuse to give up the coin. Test the amnesia by asking the child if he knows how he's going to let go of it. Then lay the larger coin in front of him and say:

I'd like to have that penny. I'll make you a trade. I'll trade you this quarter for it.

Subject may refuse with some rationalization or may make the effort to trade unsuccessfully. Urge the subject to make the trade, and then simulate impatience.

Well, I'm not going to wait all day. If you want the quarter, if you want to trade, I'll give you until I count three. If you don't want to trade before I count three, the trade is off. One.... Two....

Observe the subject's reactions. If he has tried unsuccessfully to make the trade, you have definite evidence of post-hypnotic catalepsy and amnesia. It is now time to give the signal for release so that the child can make the trade. He has earned his quarter! Scratch your head. Hold off on the number "three" until the child has observed and reacted to the release signal.

....Three. You did want it, didn't you?

Such a test is well worth the small amount of money involved. It is frequently worth much more than that to have proof positive of the depth of trance and the post-hypnotic effect. It seems rather important to permit the child to make the trade, as this helps to establish a good relationship between subject and hypnotist.

Bed wetting and nail biting are two very common symptoms of anxiety. The relief of these symptoms is definitely not a resolving of the underlying anxiety state. Whenever these symptoms are observed, psychotherapy is indicated. The symptoms themselves can frequently be permanently

176

removed with a brief series of treatments. Occasionally one treatment is enough.

One technique which has been successfully used in child dentistry and in pediatric practice consists of teaching the child to fantasy a television program. In dental practice the child is asked to watch the program and then report later; whereas the pediatrician finds it more satisfactory to ask the child to give a running account of the fantasied program as it occurs while he performs such examination or treatment as may be necessary with the child perfectly relaxed. In developing this fantasy, the therapist asks the child to look at a window and then imagine that this is a television screen. When the child has done this, he is asked to close his eyes and see the television screen in his imagination. The next step is to get him to see it in blue, then red, then yellow, then green, and then to explain to him that he is going to see a full technicolor television program. It can be his favorite program. It can be an old familiar program or a new adventure that he can compose for himself. By using the feedback method (that is, getting the child to report back on his inner experiences and then by using his own words to further fix his attention on the fantasy), the physician can insure that the fantasy is well developed before proceeding with the necessary, and sometimes otherwise unpleasant, therapeutic procedures.

BED WETTING

Hypnotize the child. Test for depth, including post-hypnotic phenomena and amnesia. Rehypnotize the child, test for depth (a hand levitation is usually adequate when amnesia has previously been induced) and continue.

Now, you are going deeper to sleep. Deeper than ever before. Deeper and deeper, deeper and deeper. You're getting to be a big boy now. You're getting to be a very big

177

boy. Soon you will be grown up. You want to grow up, don't you? If you do, nod your head.

Wait for acknowledgement. If the child indicates that he does not want to grow up, the need for psychotherapy is urgent.

Of course you do. Everybody wants to grow up. You're getting much more grown up right now, because you do what the grown-ups do. At night, when you are sleeping, you sleep all night long with a nice clean dry bed. Your bed is dry every night, and you wake up in the morning with a nice clean dry bed. You do just like the grown-ups do. If you really have to go to the toilet at night, you just get up and go to the toilet and go back to bed. If you really have to go to the toilet, you get up and go to the toilet just like the grown-ups do. But most of the time you sleep all night without wanting to get up. You go to the toilet the last thing before you go to bed every night. The last thing you do before you go to bed is to go to the toilet, just like the grown-ups do. That makes it easy for you to sleep all night long with a nice dry bed. You wake up in the morning with a nice dry bed. You wake up in the morning with a nice dry bed, just like the grown-ups do. You wake up in the morning with a nice dry bed.

NAIL-BITING

Find out which adult (parent or other) is loved and admired by the child. Find out if this person bites his nails. If the loved one is not a nail-biter, he can be used as a model. If he is a nail-biter, some other choice must be made. This must be done without directing the child's attention to nail-biting activities, probably by questioning the parents about his heros and questioning the parents about possible nail-biting on the part of the hero.

Hypnotize the child, etc., same as for bed-wetting.

Now, you're going deeper and deeper. Deeper and deeper.

Deeper than ever before. Do you love *(hero)*? If you do, nod your head.

Wait for acknowledgment.

When you grow up, do you want to be like *(hero)*?

Wait for acknowledgment.

Of course you do. Have you ever noticed what nice long, strong fingernails *(hero)* has? If you have, nod your head.

Wait for acknowledgment. If the child shakes his head, indicating that he has not noticed, follow with:

"*(hero)* does have nice long, strong fingernails. Next time you notice." *In either case, continue.*

You want to grow up to be like *(hero)*. You want to grow up with nice long, strong fingernails. You can have nice fingernails, just like *(hero)*. You are going to have nice long, strong fingernails just like *(hero)*. Your nails are growing longer and stronger right now, and they are going to keep on growing until they are long enough to file. I'll show you why they're going to grow. You simply cannot bite them any more. You try to bite your nails right now, and you will see what I mean. Try to bite them. You just can't do it.

When the child raises his hand to his mouth, let it almost touch the mouth, and then put your hand against his wrist so that he cannot get his finger into his mouth. Push the hand back down each time that he tries to bite his fingernail.

Try it again. Try to bite your fingernail.

Push hand down.

Try it again. Try with the other hand.

Push hand down.

You see, you just can't do it. You can't ever bite your fingernails any more. Now, I'll show you something funny. You can put your finger in your mouth, but you can't bite your nails. Go ahead, put your finger in your mouth.

Observe carefully. Permit the child to put the finger in

179

his mouth. If he tries to bite the nails, immediately push the hand away.

You see, you can put your finger in your mouth but you can't bite your nails. Try it again. You just can't do it.

Observe carefully. The instant the child makes the attempt to bite, push his hand down.

You see, it is now impossible for you to bite your nails. That's wonderful. That was a little baby habit, that you used to have, but you don't have it any more. You are growing up, and your nails are getting long and strong, just like *(hero)*. Your nails are growing longer and stronger every day. You're growing up now. Your nails are growing longer and stronger every day. Your nails are growing long and strong, long and strong, long and strong.

CHAPTER XXIII

SELF-CONFIDENCE

Many patients with character disorders manifest a lack of confidence in their own ability tò meet situations, make decisions, or enter into social functions. General suggestions toward the building of self-confidence can have a specific supportive value. The effect of such suggestions can be increased by an analysis of the patient's personal and social "assets," many of which remain unrealized or severely depreciated by the patient himself.

In constructing such suggestions, it is advisable first to draw out an expression of the patient's opinion of himself. Many a beautiful woman regards herself as plain or unattractive. Many a handsome man considers himself ugly.

Patients who have specific and unchangeable handicaps frequently concentrate on their liabilities, and pay little attention to their potential or actual assets. Some of the assets which may be looked for are beauty (or lack of ugliness) of face, figure, hair, etc., quality of voice, intelligence, physical condition, athletic ability, appearance of poise, knowledge, education, earning ability, professional skill, artistic ability, music, painting, drawing, acting, etc., artistic appreciation and knowledge, past accomplishments.

The therapy can begin with a waking discussion of assets and liabilities, after which the patient may be given the general suggestion for poise and confidence. To these may be added the specific suggestions for self-realization and unconscious acceptance of assets which have been deprecciated or ignored.

FOR THE DOCTOR

Hynotize the subject as deeply as possible. Light trance is adequate for this type of suggestion, but the deeper the trance the more rapid and positive is the reaction.

Go deeper and deeper to sleep. Deeper and deeper, deeper and deeper. As you go deeper, you are realizing perhaps for the first time that you are a grown person with the strength and ability that has come with your years. You are acquiring confidence in yourself. You feel growing within you a realization of the fact that you have the ability to handle any situation that you may meet. You have confidence in your ability to make decisions wisely. You make these decisions after considering the consequences of your decisions. Once you have made a decision, you rest content in the knowledge that you have made a wise decision. You dismiss it from your mind. You have confidence in your ability to make decisions wisely.

You are flexible in your decisions. You make each decision in the light of your best present knowledge. You are content with that decision when you make it. If you acquire new knowledge, you have the ability to make a new decision in light of the new knowledge. You have confidence in your decisions.

You have friends. These friends are attracted to you because of your personality. You have confidence in your ability to win and hold friends. You look upon each new acquaintance as a possible friend. You like people and people like you. It is easy for you to make friends. You have confidence in your ability to meet people and make friends. *(Repeat last sentence about three times.)*

You have many social assets. In meeting new people you are confident that they will be interested in you. You are interested in the new people that you meet. You are confident in any social situation. You are confident of your ability to join a group and become a part of that group. You are confident of your ability to contribute something to the group and to accept and enjoy the contributions of others.

You have confidence in your ability to enjoy yourself at a party, or gathering. You are confident in entering the room. You are confident in your own appearance. You are confident and poised. You know that you are going to have a good time. You are confident in joining the activities. You are confident in dancing. You are confident in asking for a dance. You are confident in accepting a friendly offer. You are confident when participating in games. You have the ability to mix with the group. You talk freely to those about you. You listen with interest when they talk. You are really interested in the people that you meet. You are interested in their personalities. You are interested in their viewpoints. You are interested in people. You have confidence in your ability to join a party and have fun.

The following special suggestions will apply according to the economic status and the sex of the patient.

1. For the husband who is working.

You have confidence in your ability to provide a good living for your family. You have confidence on the job. You have confidence in your ability to improve yourself and to increase your earnings. You have confidence in your ability to handle greater responsibilities when you are ready for them. You have confidence in your ability to make your marriage a successful marriage. You have confidence in your ability to grow closer to your wife (and family) as the years go by. You have confidence in your ability to make and keep a home.

2. For the wife who is not working.

You have confidence in your ability to back up your husband in making a good home. You have confidence in your ability to grow closer to your husband as the years go by.

You have confidence in your ability to make your home an ideal home for yourself and your husband (and family). You have confidence that as time goes on, you and your husband will grow closer and closer. You have a strong desire to develop your own interests—some of which you share with your husband—and you have the utmost confidence in your ability to grow with him, mentally as well as physically.

3. For the single man or woman who is working.

You have confidence in your ability to provide a good living for yourself and to build for the future. You have confidence in your ability on the job. You have confidence in your ability to improve yourself and increase your earnings. You have confidence in your ability to handle greater responsibilities when you are ready for them. You are confident in meeting men and women. You are confident in social situations. You are confident in approaching companions of either sex. You are confident in meeting new acquaintances of either sex.

In the following, use the applicable word, man or woman, male or female, etc.

It is becoming especially easy for you to make desirable acquaintances with the opposite sex. You meet men (women) more easily than ever before. You are interested in each man (woman) that you meet. You accept easily the friendly greetings of men (women). You are open to new experiences. You realize that the natural way of life is for a man and a woman to meet, to love, to marry, to build a home and have children. You have confidence in your ability to meet a man (woman) with whom you will fall in love, and who will fall in love with you. You accept yourself as a lovable person. You have confidence in your ability to give and to receive love.

You realize that as you increase your circle of friendship, sooner or later you will meet a man (woman) to whom you

184

will be more strongly attracted, and who will be strongly attracted to you. Eventually, you will meet the person with whom you can form a lifelong love relationship. You have confidence in your ability to meet such a person and form a marriage.

4. *For the student.*

You have confidence in your intelligence. You have confidence in your ability to master your studies. When you listen, you listen intently, and you remember what you hear. When you read, you read with an absolute concentration, and you remember what you read. You are confident of your ability to complete your school work. You are confident that you will pass with the grades you need, because you have the ability to do the work, the ability to pay close attention to what is said, the ability to concentrate when you are reading, and the ability to remember what you have heard and read.

5. *For the student who is about to take examinations.*

You have studied the material for this course, haven't you? *(Wait)* You have done the required work, haven't you? *(Wait)* You have read the required reading, haven't you? *(Wait)*

Unless you get a nod of the head for each of these questions, the suggestion must be revised to provide for rapid reading, concentration, retentive memory, etc., to facilitate "cramming."

All right, then. You know that every experience that you have ever had has left its trace in your mind. Some of these things are buried deep in the "unconscious," but you know that with hypnosis we can go back and recover them. There is in your mind a record of everything that you have ever heard or read or thought or felt or done. Now, we are going to make all of the material that you have studied available to you during the examination period.

While you are reviewing, your concentration on your

185

books, notes, and so forth will be absolute. When you sit down to read, decide how long you want to work. Write the time down on a piece of paper. As soon as you have done that, you will concentrate on your reviewing. Your concentration will be so great that nothing can disturb you unless it is absolutely necessary. Your concentration will be perfect until the time that you have written. During this time you will read rapidly and accurately, with full understanding. It is necessary for you to read only once, because this reading serves only to bring to the upper layers of your mind the studies that you have already mastered.

When you go to the examination, you are completely confident of your ability to write a perfect examination paper. You know the subject. You know that you know the subject. You are calm and self-possessed. When the questions are presented, you read them one by one. Read all the questions before attempting to answer any. You have the knowledge to answer all the questions correctly. As you read the first one, you are sending an order down to the unconscious mind. This order is that the full and correct answer be delivered from the unconscious up to your conscious memory. Sometimes this takes a little while. As you are reading the second and following questions, the answer to the first will be working up to the memory level, and at the same time you will be sending down orders for the answers to the other questions. By the time you have finished reading all the questions, you will be fully ready to answer the first one. By the time you have answered the first one, you will be ready to answer the second fully and correctly, and so on down the line. If, for any reason, the answer to a question is a little slow in being delivered, pass the question, and go on to the next one. Your second reading of the question will reinforce the order, and by the time you have finished all of the questions which come easily, the answers to the more difficult questions will be ready for you. Remember that usually the

186

last question counts as much as the first. Never wait for the answer to a question until you have answered ALL the ones that you can answer easily.

You are calm, poised, and self-confident throughout the entire examination. Because you are calm and self-confident, you work with the highest possible efficiency, and do it easily. You are calm and relaxed throughout the entire examination, and when it is over you are confident of your grades.

STAGE FRIGHT—SELF-CONSCIOUSNESS
For the Doctor

Condition the patient in hypnotic response, the deeper the better. If light responses only are achievable, this type of suggestion can work if sufficiently repeated. The patient should be cautioned (while awake) not to expect instantaneous and complete success. It may be pointed out that the patient is now responding to light trance suggestions, but is not yet able to accept those suggestions for which the deeper trance is necessary. It should be stressed that the failure of any single suggestion to be effective is not "failure." When the subject is hypnotized to his deepest level, proceed as follows:

You like people. You enjoy the company of other people. You enjoy doing things for people. You enjoy making people happy. Other people sense this feeling in you. People are aware that you like them, and they return the feeling. People like you. People enjoy your company. People like to listen to you. You are at ease when you are with people. When you stand before an audience you are filled with feelings of friendliness for them. You feel their friendliness to you. You experience a feeling of warmth, sympathy, and fellowship radiating from the members of the audience to you. You have the feeling that they are on your side. You, in turn, feel friendly to them. You are interested in them. You wish to do things for them. You are so interested in

187

them that you feel a sense of personal friendship with every member of your audience. Your sense of friendship is so great that talking (singing, acting, etc.) to these people is just like talking (singing, acting, etc.) to the one who loves you best in all this world. In this situation you are perfectly poised, self-possessed and free in your expression. You feel at ease. You enjoy doing this for your friends. You are having a very enjoyable time. You are having fun. You are having lots of fun. You find the same satisfaction in this act that you find in doing a favor for the one you love best. You are so much at ease, and you have so much fun that, automatically, you are relaxed, poised, calm. Your lips are flexible. Your mouth is moist. Your breathing is deep, from the diaphragm. Your hands are poised and calm. The gestures flow spontaneously and freely. Your legs are strong beneath you. You are comforted and peaceful. You are secure and confident in this situation. Your eyes automatically travel over the audience with a sparkle, and there is a smile in your heart which comes to your lips spontaneously at the proper times.

If the conditioning is aimed at a special single appearance, this may be followed with:

(*Tomorrow night, etc.—indicate time*) before you are introduced you will feel this friendliness and sympathy for your audience. As you are introduced you feel their warmth and friendship projected at you. You are absolutely confident. You are perfectly at ease. When you have been introduced and start to talk (sing, act, etc.), you are master of the situation. You have the undivided attention of the audience, and it makes you feel perfectly at ease and perfectly poised. You perform freely, fluidly, and perfectly. You perform with spontaneity, and with a full release of your skill, talents. When the performance is ended, and your audience applauds, you feel warm and gratified. When you are congratulated, and people wish to speak to you after your performance, you are poised, gracious, and self-confident. You thoroughly enjoy the whole evening.

For the Patient

The doctor's suggestion for overcoming self-consciousness, given to a deep trance subject, will frequently produce amazing release of the personality. When used with light trance subjects it is best to repeat it a number of times to build up the feeling within the patient. If the subject has responded to the medium trance stage, it is highly advisable to teach the subject autohypnosis. (See Chapter X). When the subject has learned the techniques of self-inducing, testing, and awakening from the trance, and has been taught the use of symbols, the suggestion for self-administration may be formulated like this:

POISED

is the key word for the following suggestion: I am poised, spontaneous, and free in all of my contacts with other human beings. I am especially poised when I am before the public. When I am being introduced I feel a wave of sympathy, understanding and friendship for my entire audience. As I am introduced, I feel their friendship radiating toward me. I perform flawlessly, confidently, and enjoy the act of performing. I am poised, and am master of the situation at all times. My lips are flexible, my mouth is moist. I breathe deeply from the diaphragm. My hands are poised and calm. The gestures flow spontaneously and freely. My legs are strong beneath me. I am secure and confident. My eyes automatically travel over the audience, searching out my friends in the farthest rows. There is a smile within me which spontaneously comes to my lips at the proper times. When my performance is concluded, I am warm and gratified by the applause. I talk graciously and with full self-confidence to those who congratulate me after the performance. I have a thoroughly enjoyable time. The whole idea is symbolized by the thought: POISED

189

CHAPTER XXIV

CONCENTRATION

AND RETENTIVE MEMORY

Hypnotize the patient to the medium trance stage or deeper.

Go deeper and deeper to sleep, deeper and deeper to sleep, deeper and deeper, deeper and deeper. It is possible for people to concentrate so strongly when reading, studying, or working that they are completely unaware of things that happen around them. Have you ever seen anyone like that? Have you ever said something to a person who is reading or working and have him fail to hear you? If you have, nod your head.

Wait. If the subject does not nod his head, ad lib with examples of concentration which might have been observed by the subject. Do this until you gain a nod as recognition of some situation in which the subject has observed deep concentration.

Then you know that such concentration is possible. If you know that such concentration is possible, nod your head. *(Wait)* It is possible for you to concentrate like that. Perhaps you remember some time in your life when you were so interested in some one particular thing that you became oblivious to everything else. If you can remember such a time, nod your head.

Wait. If the subject does not answer this one, point out that his experience in going into a hypnotic trance is a type of concentration, which is similar to the one described. Continue until you obtain a nod of affirmation.

190

In your experience of learning to be hypnotized you have developed a high degree of ability to concentrate your attention. Your attention is concentrated on me right now. Perhaps you are aware of the things that are happening outside or around you, but they simply do not matter. You are concentrating. You already have the ability to concentrate when you get hypnotized. You're beginning to realize that you have this ability to concentrate. You are beginning to feel a sense of confidence in your ability to concentrate. You realize that if you can concentrate to this extent in going into hypnosis, you can concentrate on your work, your reading, and on your studies in exactly the same way but without being hypnotized. If you understand this, nod your head.

Wait. It is important to gain the subject's affirmative response to each of these steps. If the subject cannot respond to any of the suggested situations, say, ("You are going to remember some example of the type of thing that I am talking about. We will wait while ideas come to you. Soon you will realize that you know of an example. When you do, raise your right hand") *Sometimes such a vague and nondirective suggestion will enable the subject to furnish his own example.*

From now on, when you wish to concentrate, get ready for the work that you are going to do. Get your book or books, writing materials, or the tools with which you are going to work, and have them all ready for the job to be done. Look at the clock or your watch and decide how long you wish to concentrate. Then say to yourself aloud three times the *time* at which you wish to break this concentration. For example, if it is eight-thirty in the evening, and you wish to study or write until eleven o'clock, get ready and then say to yourself aloud, ELEVEN, ELEVEN, ELEVEN. As you say those words you will begin to concentrate. Your thoughts will start to narrow down to the job at hand. Your ears will start to become less sensitive to surrounding noises. Your eyes will be drawn to the work you are about to do. Start working. If it is reading, start reading. If it is writing, start writing. Whatever the job is, start doing it. Within the next few minutes, your attention increases until you are oblivious of your surroundings. In the next few minutes the rest of the world seems to fade away, so that for you there exists only the job at hand and you who are doing that job. The concentration rapidly becomes perfect and remains that way until the time that you have stated aloud. Your concentration is unbroken unless there is some real and necessary reason for you to attend to other things. Your concentration is continuous and perfect from a few minutes after you start working until the time you have set yourself. Until the time comes that you stated aloud, your thoughts are all directed toward the job at hand. The outside world is far away. Your concentration is perfect. Your concentration is absolutely perfect until the time you have set yourself. Do you understand this perfectly? Is this clear in your mind? If you understand what you are to do, and how it will work, please nod your head.

Wait. If the subject does not nod his head, ask him to tell you the points on which he is not clear, and discuss these points with him until he is fully satisfied that he understands.

The knowledge that you gain by reading, studying, observing, or by any work that you do in this concentrated way remains in your conscious memory much longer. As you read, study, or work in this manner, you will find your ability to remember facts, principles, details, theories and general trends increasing.

You retain a perfect conscious memory of the material that you acquire in this way. You are also and simultaneously acquiring a new ability to remember things that you have previously forgotten. Your mind has an association pattern for everything that has happened to you. Theoretically, it

192

is possible for you to remember every thought, feeling, and sensation that has occurred since you were born. Theoretically, it is possible for you to remember every word that you have ever read.

We might consider the mind to be like a library. The mind of a very young child is like the library of a person who owns a few books. These books are all on the table, all available. As the child grows older and has more experiences, his mind is like the library of a very well read man. Some of the current books are on the table, available for instant use. Others are in the bookcase, and it may take a little time to find a particular book. Some may be up in the attic and the owner has even forgotten their titles. It would take a little longer to find one of these books.

By the time we reach maturity, our minds can be compared to a great public library. Some books which represent our current experience and the well-remembered facts of our past are on the public shelves. A great many more are in the storage files. We can get these books but we have to wait a little while. We have to send in an order, and soon the book comes back. Those books represent the memories which are just below the conscious level. Then, of course, there are the books at the bindery, the books stored away in the basement storage rooms, and some which are locked in the vaults. These represent the deeply repressed memories which are more difficult to recover. All these books are available to us. Some we can pick off the shelves at our convenience. Some we must send for, and we must wait while they come. Some are not usually available, but we can get them if we are willing to work a little harder and wait a little longer.

Most of the memories that will be useful to you are either in the consciousness—that is, the public shelves—or just below the conscious level—that is, the reserve shelves. The ones that concern you most are the ones in the reserve shelves. As your concentration grows more perfect, your conscious memory is tremendously increased. You have a great many more books on the public shelves than ever were there before. Memories stay in the consciousness longer. You are also acquiring a better system for pulling memories up out of the unconscious.

Perhaps in the past you have fumed and fretted when you could not remember something. Perhaps you have sent an order into the unconscious, an order to deliver that memory, but you have not waited for the memory to be delivered. You have TRIED to remember, and that is the wrong method. From now on, when you wish information that you have previously known, look first on the public shelves. Possibly you remember it. If it isn't there, send an order into the unconscious. Tell yourself that you want to remember. Tell yourself clearly and specifically as though you were ordering a book at the library. Actually form the thoughts, or, if possible, say aloud, "I wish to remember Bill Smith's phone number," "I want the memory of the capitals of the forty-eight states," "I wish to remember the formula for quadratic equations," and so forth. If it is not possible to say it aloud, SAY it to yourself. Think it clearly. Then dismiss that particular matter from your mind. Let your mind do other things. Fuming and fretting will NOT hurry the memory, but it may prevent it from coming at all. When you have placed the order, wait patiently, and the memory will soon be delivered. Do you understand this clearly? If so, please nod your head.

Wait, and, if necessary, clarify this concept with ad lib discussion.

CHAPTER XXV

NON-DIRECTIVE USE OF HYPNOSIS

The patient has within himself the potential for his own healing.

This is not a new idea. But it is only in recent years that leaders in the field of hypnoanalytic therapy, like leaders in the non-hypnotic forms of psychotherapy, have developed techniques which make use of this concept.

Implicit in the ability of the individual to "cure" himself is the dynamic consideration that he caused the condition in the first place. Here we have the entire paraphernalia of repressed (fogotten) traumatic material, wherein the individual has successfully eliminated a shock experience of the past from his foreconsciousness, but is simultaneously permitting it to damage him below the level of his awareness. It has been reasonably well established that many psychosomatic conditions, phobias and other maladaptive actions are rooted in just such "forgotten experiences.

One of the advantages of hypnosis is the speed with which the repressed traumatic material can be brought up to the level of consciousness, remembered, re-experienced, and relieved of its emotional content. As Watkins[34] has shown, the use of hypnosis for this purpose has proved successful when applied to the trauma of recent war experiences. In a more general way, Wolberg[37] has illustrated at length the uses of age regression and "re-experiencing."

It is not the intention of the authors to elaborate on the

methods mentioned in the foregoing paragraphs. Even when accelerated by the use of hypnosis, the techniques of depth psychology and analysis are usually too time consuming for the general practitioner. However, there are occasions when a problem cannot be avoided. The following is an example of such an instance.

A physician brought his 25-year-old nurse to a psychologist for training in hypnotic anaesthesia. His plan was to have her acquire an understanding of the process and techniques, so that she would be able to assist him with obstetrical patients. One method of making a genuine test of the extent of anaesthesia is by probing the individual with a sterilized needle.

The nurse showed reluctance to being tested in this way, so the psychologist made use of her previous conditioning in deep trance hypnosis to do a brief psychotherapy on this particular phobia. The technique which was used is partially reproduced below. It will be readily seen that it is impossible to devise a word-for-word process that would be applicable in any situation. However, the structure, as given in this case, is applicable. The technique, as printed in the following pages, should be regarded as a guide, an indication of the way the therapist would operate.

As soon as the phobia was resolved (as shown in detail below) the psychologist continued with the technique of teaching anaesthesia, as given in Chapter XVIII.

LOCATING AND DESENSITIZING
A SPECIFIC PHOBIA

Hypnotize the patient to the deepest possible level.
Please note the initial words spoken to the patient are directive, as differentiated from the non-directive method of the later material. Directive statements such as these are based upon the psychologist's wide experience with

196

people and their problems. For the sake of saving time, the psychologist states what he believes will be acceptable to the patient, and then goes on to the main task of the process, which is dealt with non-directively.

Therapist: You were not born with the fear of being stuck by a needle. As a nurse, you have used needles many times on many patients, and you know that not all of your patients are afraid. You learned to be afraid of needles at some time in the past, probably when you were a little girl. Your unconscious mind knows why you are afraid of needles. Your unconscious mind knows when you learned to be afraid of needles. I am going to ask your unconscious mind to help you to understand why you have been afraid of needles. I am going to ask your right hand to float up into the air from the couch on which it is resting, and to float over and touch your face. As your hand floats up, I am going to ask your unconscious mind to give you a memory, or a dream, or a thought, or an idea, which will have some connection with your fear of being stuck by a needle. The hand will now get light, and float up toward your face. It will not touch your face until your unconscious mind has given you some material connected with your fear of needles.

WAIT. If the hand is extremely slow in moving, or if you are dealing with a patient who has not had previous experience with hand levitation, it may be necessary to use some of the wording of paragraph 31, Chapter II. When the hand touches the face, continue:

Therapist: Do you have some kind of a memory?
Patient: Yes. I got a splinter in my foot.
T.:   How old were you?
P.:   Eight, I think."
T.:   Can you tell me what happened?
P.:   I got a splinter in my foot. Mother tried to take it

out, but she couldn't get it all, so we had to go to the doctor. It hurt terribly.

T.: Where did you get the splinter?

P.: I got it on the front porch. We were saying goodbye to some friends.

T.: All right, now, *be* on the front porch. Feel the porch with your bare feet. Where is mother standing? At your right, your left, or behind you?

P.: She's at my right.

T.: Now, live through it again.

The patient was quiet for a short time, and then began to twist on the couch. Finally, she cried out:

P.: Oh, mother, it hurts.

T.: That's right. Feel the hurt. Feel it as much as you can. Here, squeeze my hand.

Therapist grasps the patient's right hand firmly with his own.

T.: When it hurts very much, you squeeze my hand harder. Now, let's go back to the porch, and live through it again.

P.: Oh, no, it hurts too much.

T.: Where are you?

P.: In the bathroom.

T.: Are you? Whose hand are you squeezing?

P.: Yours.

T.: Where are you?

P.: In your office.

T.: Is there really a splinter in your foot right now?

P.: No, not really, but it hurts.

T.: Sure, it hurts. But it's just the memory of a hurt. You can stand it, can't you?

P.: I guess so.

T.: All right, go back to the porch, wave goodbye to the people, and feel the splinter go into your foot again.

This time the patient re-lived the experience of mother probing for the splinter, recalled mother's conversation at the time when all of the splinter could not be removed, and then re-lived the experience of going to the doctor's office with her, and re-lived the doctor's probing. The doctor commented that the splinter went all the way to the bone. The patient displayed much anguish while re-living the experience with the doctor, who used no anaesthetic. When the doctor finished, she sighed with relief, and said:

P.:   It doesn't hurt any more.

T.:   Now, go back to the porch, and wave goodbye to the people again.

WAIT.

T.:   How does it feel this time? Does it hurt more, less, or the same?

P.:   It doesn't hurt so much this time, hardly at all.

T.:   Feel all the hurt that there is. Feel it as much as you can. Tell me when you finish at the doctor's office.

WAIT.

P.:   He's all through now.

T.:   Did it hurt much this time?

P.:   Hardly at all when mother tried to get it out. But it still hurt when the doctor was working on me.

T.:   All right, go back to the porch, and go through the whole experience again. You can go faster where there is absolutely no hurt left, but be sure to go slow and feel all of the pain wherever there is any left.

WAIT.

P.:   It's all over now.

T.:   Did you get much pain?

P.:   Hardly any.

T.:   Go through it again, and get it *all.*

WAIT.

P.:   I couldn't feel any pain this time.

T.: Good. Now, I'm going to ask you to give me a hunch answer. You can't know this intellectually, but your unconscious mind can give you a feeling about it. Were you ever afraid of needles before this?

P.: (after a pause) No.

T.: All right. From that experience up to the present time a few minutes ago, before we hypnotized you, there have been various times in your life when you have been stuck by needles, or afraid of needles. I want you to start with this experience that we have just had, the one with the splinter, and grow older quite rapidly. As you do this, take a quick look at each new experience that comes to your mind between then and now. In each case, feel the pain or the fear of needles. When you have lived through these experiences, including your fear before we started this hypnosis, please let me know.

P.: (after about two minutes) I'm not afraid of them any more.

In the above case, the patient quickly produced a detailed memory with full imagery. In working with phobias, compulsions and other areas of tension, which are of greater magnitude than the one shown, the repression is frequently so great that such a direct approach is not possible. Notice that in the first instruction to the patient, she was told that she might have a memory or a dream or a thought or an idea. Frequently, a patient will produce some kind of dream material with a symbolism which may be anything from very transparent to extremely obscure. In some instances, the patient will be able to interpret his own dream almost immediately. In other instances, the usual techniques of dream analysis must be employed.

One of the ways in which a dream may be analyzed is to direct the patient to dream again about the same material, using a different and less obscure symbolism. This may be repeated a number of times, with the symbolism progressively changing until the patient gets the clue to a real experience of the past. The experience can then be de-sensitized by "re-living" it, as was done in the example described above. It is worthy of note that the patient—in the example —was not completely age-regressed. There was, except for a short time, an awareness of the reality of the present surroundings, and of the therapist. On occasion, a patient will become completely age-regressed, and will re-live the incident without awareness of the present time surroundings. If this happens, contact with the present can be re-established as it was in the above case. The therapeutic value in such an experience seems to lie in recapturing the emotion of the experience *while* maintaining an awareness of the present. Thus discrimination between the past and the present is achieved.

How complete is de-sensitization, once related experiences have been de-sensitized? In the example, the patient was awakened from the hypnosis, and handed a sterilized needle. She was able to test her own sensitivity to the needle prick on the ball of her thumb without fear and without flinching.

It is important to emphasize that it is not always possible to eliminate an individual's phobia by the re-living of a single incident. It may be necessary to use the same technique on a series of experiences. Sometimes, the first experience offered will be a so-called "cover memory," and when the pain and fear of this initial experience are relieved, an earlier and more deeply repressed experience will be available. This, and subsequent experiences which successively show themselves, should be dealt with, and usually the phobia will not be permanently resolved until they have been de-sensitized. It is obvious that such progressively deeper probing may require more time than many practitioners are able to devote.

The therapist must be prepared for emotional outbursts

on the part of the patient. Tears and screams are frequently encountered. Rage may be expressed verbally or by striking out. It is helpful to have a pillow or cushion handy to be struck, or choked, or kicked by the patient. In such circumstances, the therapist must retain his composure, and express it verbally by encouraging remarks. For example, if the patient starts to cry: "Go ahead and cry." "That's good." "Scream as loud as you want to." In handing him a pillow, say: "Here, choke him, or punch his nose in."

Do not show any amazement, or criticism of emotional outbursts on the part of the patient. The acting out of emotion relieves a great deal of internal stress for the patient.

CHAPTER XXVI

THE USE OF INTERNAL AWARENESS

Emotions produce muscular and glandular changes in the body. For example, a person suffering from the chronic emotion of fear usually suffers from chronic muscular contractions, in that he has a tight diaphragm, a stiff neck, or tight shoulders. Sometimes he complains of a lump in the throat. Frequently, he has come to regard these contractions as "normal," and he feels comfortable only when he is in a tense position, whereas the fact is that maintaining these tensions saps his energy. As Hans Selye has demonstrated, chronic stress situations produce chronic changes in the structure and function of the adrenal glands, and in the vascular system.

Hypnotists of the older style, when dealing with a person manifesting such tensions, usually began by teaching the patient how to achieve an hypnotic trance. And then, when the ability to go into trance had been attained, they utilized suggestion to relieve the physical tensions that accompanied the fear state. Generally speaking, the authors recommend such a division of techniques, and indeed this work is constructed to utilize an approach that begins with training in hypnosis, after which specific therapy techniques are to be used.

However, the non-directive hypnotherapist has in recent years learned how to use the physiological reactions of the various emotions to achieve the hypnotic trance. He can also direct the attention to muscular tensions as a means of uncovering emotions which are not labeled or recognized by the patient for what they really are.

Two of the more common psychological symptoms which

can be picked up in this way, and utilized to induce hypnosis, are fear and the necessity for "self-control." What makes this particularly useful is that virtually every patient who may be in need of psychotherapy suffers from expressed or suppressed fear.

Where the fear is suppressed—i.e., where the patient knows he is afraid but suppresses outward reaction of it—the technique may be used as early as the first session. What is more, it can be used as a disguised technique, and can be handled so subtly in this fashion that the patient need never know that he has been hypnotized.

BODY AWARENESS
FOR THE FEARFUL PATIENT

The following case history is that of a woman, age 35, mother of three children, who was making a poor adjustment to her husband. Her original attack of panic had occurred about three years previously. She had become progressively more fearful in public places and public situations. She reached the point where she could not, and indeed refused to, ride anywhere in an automobile. For a year she had found it impossible to walk to the large grocery store three blocks from her home to purchase the grocery needs of her family. She even felt uncomfortable and exposed while standing in her own front yard.

She was referred to an hypnotherapist by a physician. At the time of the referral, the woman's field of activity was confined to her home and a fenced-in back yard; and so, the physician requested that the therapist see her at her home.

The first interview took place with the patient seated on a davenport. The therapist sat beside her, and her youngest child, a three year old daughter, was present throughout the discussion. She described the symptoms and general background of her condition, repeating much of what the physician had already told the therapist, of her panic in

204

public situations of any kind, particularly her extreme fear of riding in an automobile.

The discussion turned to her family background, and it was quickly apparent that she felt extremely antagonistic to her mother-in-law, who was of a different religious faith, and who was unrelenting in her attempts to convert the patient. Shortly after mentioning her mother-in-law, she said: "I have the most awful knot in the pit of my stomach."

At this point, the therapist used the following technique:

Please note that no preliminary training is used for this technique. The woman has reported that the pit of her stomach feels knotted up. The therapist simply takes it from there.

Therapist: Please close your eyes, lean back against the couch, and feel the knot in your stomach. Put all your attention on it. Feel it as much as you can.

Patient: When you say, feel it, do you mean, be aware of it?

T.: That's right. Don't try to do anything about it. Just feel what is there.

WAIT ABOUT ONE MINUTE

T.: How does it feel now, stronger, less strong, or the same?

P.: It feels worse.

T.: That's fine. Just keep on feeling it.

WAIT ABOUT ONE MINUTE

T.: How does it feel now, worse, better, or the same?

P.: Oh, it feels much better now. But I feel so silly. I feel as if I want to cry.

T.: If you want to cry, go right ahead. There's nothing silly about it. Sometimes, it makes one feel much better.

That is the technique. "Feel it." "Continue to feel it." It may seem surprising that so little can accomplish so much, but in fact this is an outstanding method of relieving emotional stress. It should be noted that the therapist must be confident, and unhurried, and show understanding. He must be aware that a direct use can be made of this technique only with individuals who are willing to admit their fear. With a little experience, the neo-therapist will come to recognize these differences, and will therefore be able to add this tool to his repertoire of techniques.

In the case described above, the patient burst into tears almost as soon as the therapist told her that it was all right for her to cry. She wept with hard sobs while the therapist occasionally encouraged her by saying: "That's fine." Or "This is very good for you." The mother's tears brought a reaction from the three-year-old daughter. She walked around in front of her mother, and stood there with an interested but puzzled expression on her face. A few reassuring words from the therapist seemed to satisfy her, and she became merely curious.

The patient sobbed for at least five minutes, at which time she controlled herself, and began to apologize, remarking that she "never cried." She also commented that she felt as if a great weight had been lifted from her, and that she felt better than she had felt in a year.

Altogether, the therapist visited this woman in her home six times, each time using principally and in a sustained fashion the same technique for releasing emotion. At this point she felt able to go to the therapist's office, which she did, arriving however in a state of almost complete collapse. As was to be expected she had suffered from acute panic throughout most of the drive. Much of the two-hour session was spent in partially regressing her, and helping her to relive the drive. The method for doing this was illustrated in the chapter on Non-Directive Use of Hypnosis, wherein the nurse was relieved of her phobia against being pricked by a needle. The balance of the time was used in the same manner working on previous panics which the patient experienced while riding in a car.

In subsequent sessions, this patient learned to associate certain of her physical tensions with the emotion of fear. The principal tension always appeared in the diaphragm, and there was usually a tension in the throat. As often happens, this patient became perceptive of her reactions while in therapy and she was able to report fear manifestations almost as soon as they appeared. Whether she was talking about a problem in her current life, or whether she was regressed to a traumatic episode in her earlier life, the moment she reported that fear was building up, the therapist would revert to the above technique, and instruct her to "feel the fear."

It was established many times that this of course meant that she should feel the physical manifestations which accompanied the emotion of fear. What happened then usually followed a definite pattern. As she concentrated her attention on the area of tensions, and on the feeling of fear, she would become more aware of them, and thus the tightness, pain, "lump" or "knot" would seem to increase. Often, this intensification would be maintained for several minutes, but slowly the muscles relaxed, and presently the patient reported the disappearance of the fear manifestations and of the feeling of fear.

With this particular patient, the techniques of depth psychology were so augmented by this specific method of desensitizing fear that, within two months, she was doing her own grocery shopping. After five months (in this case, 40 hours of therapy), she secured her driver's license, and started driving the family automobile. Therapy continued for a total of 11 months (88 hours), at the end of which time she felt able to continue a normal life without further psychotherapy.

BODY AWARENESS
FOR THE SELF-CONTROLLED PERSON

Not everyone recognizes the emotional pattern that lies

behind their tensions. For such individuals, it is a necessary part of the therapy that the patient be helped to recognize the connection between physical tensions and emotional states. This is sometimes difficult to do, because many people have reacted to unendurable pressures in their environments by "shutting off" the sensations in their bodies, and by denying emotions (such as fear or anger). It becomes a part of the person's so-called "defense mechanism" that he cannot admit, for the sake of his self-respect, that he is capable of feeling such emotions in life situations. Such an individual must be taught, as non-directively as possible, to label the emotions of fear, grief, anger, hatred, hopelessness, disgust, guilt and shame. When he reaches the stage where he can be aware that he does feel emotions, this recognition will frequently, in itself, bring relief for some of his symptoms. Once this stage is reached, more rapid gains are possible, because the technique—which has already been illustrated—may now be used without encountering lack of comprehension or resistance. Once the connection between physical tensions and emotions is accepted by the patient, the therapist need merely say: "Feel the fear," or "feel the shame," or "feel the anger," etc.

The goal is to bring the individual to the stage where such a direct and simple approach may be utilized. The following account, it will be found, illustrates closely the reaction a therapist will run into, and also illustrates what he should do about it. The verbal pattern may be paralleled almost precisely for most cases.

As with the technique for the fearful patient, this technique for the self-controlled person may be used on a first interview, and it can be used as a disguised technique. It is probably most effective when the patient is on a couch, or on a treatment table. But it can be used with the patient sitting in a reclining type of chair. A good beginning for this method is for the therapist to ask the patient to relax.

*In the example which follows, the patient responded to the
request to relax by assuming a position wherein his knees
pressed tightly together, his ankles were crossed, and he
clasped his hands tightly over his abdomen. During the entire therapy period, the patient reclined on a couch.*

*To recapitulate, the therapist first asked the patient to
relax. Then he noticed the position which the patient assumed. Then:*

Therapist: Please notice the feelings in your body. Send
your attention from the tip of your toes to the top of your
head, and tell me what you feel.

Patient: (after a pause) Nothing.

Therapist: By nothing do you mean, painful. Or just
nothing?

Patient: Just nothing.

Therapist: Please raise your right hand like this——

*Adjust the patient's hand and arm, so that is is held ver-
tically at his side, with the elbow resting on the couch.*

Therapist: Now, put your attention on your hand. Feel
your hand. What do you feel?

Patient: Nothing.

Therapist: Please close your eyes. Now, do you know
where your hand is? No, don't wiggle it, or move it. Just
feel it. Can you tell where it is, and that it is there, by feeling it? Or do you just remember that it was there when
you closed your eyes? How do you know you have a hand?

Patient: I can feel it.

Therapist: What do you feel?

Patient: Oh, a kind of tingling.

Therapist: That is what I mean. If you notice carefully,
you can feel the life processes going on in every part of your
body. Now, please put your hand wherever you wish to, and
feel your body from head to foot again.

WAIT.

P.: I've finished.

T.: Did you feel tight or uncomfortable in any part of your body?

P.: Yes, I noticed a little tightness in my stomach.

T.: Fine. Now, feel the tightness in your stomach. Feel it in the same way you felt the feelings in your hand.

WAIT FOR A MINUTE OR TWO.

T.: Is there any change? Do you feel the tightness more, less, or the same?

P.: It seems to be a little more.

T.: That's good. Now, keep on feeling it.

WAIT AGAIN. Let us suppose that this time, after the wait, the patient reports that the feelings have increased. This would indicate an increased awareness of the tensions. It does not mean an increase of the tensions. In the case of a self-controlled person, the therapist should realize that a great deal of tension probably exists at all times, but that the person has shut down his awareness of it. When he begins to feel the tensions, it is his awareness of them that is turning on.

The foregoing is one possibility.

Another possibility is that the patient may say that the tensions have decreased. In this instance, it is necessary for the therapist to say: "Have you been aware of it all the time, or has the feeling seemed to come and go?" Please note carefully that if the feeling has been continuously present, but decreasing, the desired result is being accomplished. On the other hand, if the feeling has seemed to come and go, with no particular change in intensity—i. e., it has been simply an on and off process—then you may assume that the patient's attention is wandering. Explain to him that it is essential for him to hold his attention on the feeling in a sustained fashion, and that no reduction of the tension will occur if he permits his mind to wander.

A third possible result of this awareness technique can be

that the feelings remain unchanged. If this is the case,
simply ask the patient to continue feeling the tension.

For some people, it is necessary to continue this process
as much as twenty or thirty minutes before the tension
dissipates.

Now, let us examine another, and further development of
the technique of awareness. The therapist simply carries on
with the technique, as has already been shown.

Therapist: How is the abdominal tension now, stronger,
less, or the same?

P.: It's gone. I feel relaxed.

T.: Fine. Now, feel your body from the tip of your toes
to the top of your head again, and see if there are any other
tensions or discomforts present.

WAIT.

P.: No, everything seems relaxed.

T.: I notice that your ankles are crossed, your knees are
pressed tightly together, and your hands are clasped together on your abdomen. I want you to change that position.
Separate your hands, and let them fall to your sides, palm
up. Uncross your ankles, and separate your feet by about
twelve inches. How does this feel?

P.: I feel uncomfortable.

T.: Where do you feel tight?

P.: In my arms and legs. It's just not a comfortable position.

T.: Evidently, it isn't for some people. And yet, a baby
will sleep perfectly relaxed in this position. So will a healthy
child. It's only when we feel the need to protect ourselves
that we cover up, and tighten up. Now, put your hands and
feet where they were, and feel how much more secure you
are in that position. Yet it is visibly a more tense position.
You are maintaining a tension in order to protect yourself
from feelings which are unpleasant to you. Now, feel—that
is, become aware—of your arms and legs and shoulders, and

211

see if you can perceive the tightness involved in maintaining the position.

WAIT.

P.: Yes, I can feel a little tightness in the legs and tightness in the arms.

T.: All right, ask yourself this question: "What am I afraid of? Why am I afraid to be relaxed?" Don't expect an answer right away, but if you ask yourself that question every time you find yourself in this position, you may get an answer in time.

WAIT

T.: Now, separate your hands and feet, and feel the anxiety that comes in this position.

WAIT.

T.: How do you feel, worse, better, or the same?

P.: I feel relaxed. It's quite comfortable now.

Frequently, feeling the tension will bring to the patient new insights into emotions which he has suppressed. It may stimulate memories of traumatic (shock) experiences, or produce a new train of thought. When the self-controlled person has learned to identify the anxiety which produces the tense posture, and the security and relaxation of the open, exposed posture, he has taken his first step toward releasing his self-control. If the awareness training continues, he will come to recognize his involuntary defensive tightening when traumatic material is approached. If his motivation towards self-improvement is strong, he can use this very signal as a means of stimulating him to face the thing he is unconsciously trying to avoid.

BODY AWARENESS
FOR A SPECIFIC PROBLEM

Many headaches are the result of body tensions. It is often possible successfully to eliminate a headache of this type by the use of a body awareness technique, as follows:

212

Therapist: Please close your eyes, and feel the headache. Where do you feel it?

Patient: At the temple, over the eyes, and at the back of the head.

T.: All right, feel it as much as you can. Keep feeling it. *30 SECOND WAIT.*

T.: How is it now, better, worse, or the same?

P.: Worse.

T.: That's good. That means you are really feeling it. You realize that normally you would be trying to do the opposite of what you are now doing. That is, you would be trying not to feel it. Continue to feel it as much as you can. Do you feel any tightness or discomfort anywhere else?

P.: No.

WAIT.

T.: How is it now, worse, better or the same?

P.: It seems to be a little better, but I can feel that my neck is tight.

The field of self-awareness is increasing, and the patient is now becoming aware of the muscular tension which accompanies the headache.

T.: Keep on feeling the headache, and also feel the tightness in the neck.

Patient moves his head from side to side.

T.: No, don't wiggle it, or stretch it. That is only putting one tight muscle against another. That simply increases the tension. Just hold still, and feel the tightness.

WAIT

T.: How is it now, worse, better or the same?

P.: The headache is lots better, and the neck is not quite so tense. But I can feel the tightness in the shoulders now.

T.: Try to feel them all at the same time, the headache, the neck tension, and the shoulder tension.

WAIT

213

P.:   Oh, it's gone now. The shoulder muscle just let go, and I don't have a headache any more. It's gone.

Since none of the usual tests were attempted in the foregoing examples, the question may well be asked: is the use of body awareness actually a hypnotic approach?   One answer is that the process of fixing the attention on the bodily sensations seems to fulfil all the requirements previously given for induction of hypnosis. It should be borne in mind that there are scores of methods which, in their beginnings, do not constitute hypnosis, but which, when carried forward by the skillful hypnotic technician, lead smoothly into the hypnotic state. Experience indicates that body awareness can be used for this purpose. In the case of patients who are extremely self-controlled, this approach may be almost the only possible way of inducing a light trance in a reasonable time. Since it is frequently advisable to conceal permanently from the self-controlled person that body awareness may be a hypnotic technique, it is obvious that tests of the ordinary type cannot be used, so that evidence in such instances must be indirect.

The evidence is that the same techniques used on persons who are less self-controlled, and who are capable of a more vivid imagery, may be followed by direct tests for depths of trance with good success.

It may therefore be assumed, though with qualifications, that the technique of internal awareness has induced light trance, or at least an hypnoidal state in the more self-controlled patient.

It is of interest to note that the technique of body awareness can be used rapidly and successfully wih a patient who is already hypnotized. It can definitely be used to induce light hypnosis in some patients. And, as has been shown, it can be used to alleviate a headache with a patient who has never before been hypnotized.

214

IN CONCLUSION

The doctor who use the therapies in this book will soon discover that the hypnotic trance depths which his patients will frequently attain, seem to offer greater opportunities for therapy than the book itself provides for. In this he is not mistaken. The use of hypnosis with psychoanalysis and other techniques of psychotherapy constitutes one of the important advances of modern therapeutic psychology.

APPENDIX

A TRAINING METHOD
FOR HYPNOTIC CHILDBIRTH

by Richard N. Clark, M. D.

APPENDIX

A TRAINING PERIOD
FOR HYPNOTIC CHILDBIRTH

After searching the literature diligently, I have been unable to find a word for word account on how to train patients for hypnotic childbirth. There are innumerable case histories where hypnosis was employed as the only analgesic agent. However, no detailed explanation is offered telling exactly how it was accomplished. It would appear that this information has been deliberately or intentionally withheld. Such a valuable and gratifying aid to obstetrical patients should be made readily available to all physicians and psychotherapists. To fill this omission, I dedicate the following chapter.

A clear understanding of the basic facts of hypnosis, by the patient, is paramount for the successful use of hypnosis in obstetrics. To this end each patient is given a leaflet containing a brief description of the uses of hypnosis in medicine. The common misunderstandings and fallacies of hypnosis are clarified. The patient is oriented, in a general way, as to what she can expect to experience while under hypnosis. Also she is told just what is expected of her, in order that she may cooperate as a good subject. The word 'Hypnosis' is used frequently in the office. I do not attempt to hide its identity under the guise of such words as, suggestive relaxation, progressive relaxation, etc. The following is a copy of the leaflet.

219

HYPNOTIC RELAXATION
AS AN AID TO CHILDBIRTH

Almost everyone would like to know how to relax easily. How pleasant life would be, if when anxiety and nervous tension develops, you could turn off an imaginary switch and allow your mind and body to relax completely. Every natural process in the body is painless when it is functioning properly. Nervous tension frequently interferes with the functions of the body. Tension in itself, can be the cause of pain; for instance, the common headache is usually caused by 'nervous tension.' Nervous tension is the basic cause of stomach ulcers and many other conditions where there is muscular spasm and tension. Anxiety, fear and nervous tension can produce heart attacks and chest pain. Also skin diseases and allergic conditions are aggravated by tension. It may come as a surprise to most people, that the discomfort of normal childbirth is almost negligible for the mother, if she is relaxed, and has no fear, anxiety, or tension. The dental chair also holds little fear for the patient who is completely relaxed. Discomfort of any type is decreased when you are relaxed, both in mind and body. Relaxation is healing; relaxation is soothing and restful.

Every woman wants her pregnancy and childbirth to be normal. The vast majority of births follow the normal and natural process. There is every reason for her to be assured that it will be normal when she is under the care of a competent doctor, in whom she has complete confidence. In childbirth the circular muscles of the lower part of the uterus relax, and allow the longitudinal muscles of the upper part of the uterus to contract and push the baby down through the birth canal. Tension may cause the circular muscles of the lower part of the uterus (the cervix) to tighten up, so that not only are labor contractions painful, but also labor may be retarded. We know that labor is hard

220

work, however, work does not need to be painful. Normal work can leave you pleasantly tired and relaxed.

Briefly then, the pain of labor is due to tension caused by fear. The pain intensifies the fear, which in turn increases the tension by resistance of the muscles. And so the vicious circle of these three evils (tension, fear and pain) destroys all confidence, relaxation and self-control.

Relaxation is the goal for which we are striving. With relaxation comes a feeling of self-control, confidence, security, contentment and well-being. The sensation of complete relaxation while you are conscious, is the identical sensation you would have if you were under hypnotic relaxation and sleep. Hypnosis helps you to relax more completely than you can by any other method. The ability to relax completely is a skill which you can easily develop with practice. Our main purpose is to decrease tension and to decrease anxiety due to the cares of everyday living.

When you close your eyes and relax completely, you are experiencing the same feelings and sensations that you will be aware of when you are under hypnosis. It is a day-dream like feeling where you are calm and relaxed. Although you are relaxed, drowsy and comfortable, you are also *definitely conscious*. You see, hypnosis is not like night sleep because with hypnotic sleep and relaxation you are *always* conscious and aware of things about you. Hypnosis is useful medically because you are conscious and you are able to cooperate and carry out suggestions that will be beneficial to you. Under hypnosis you are merely in a relaxed condition of increased suggestibility. You must be able to concentrate, and most important you must have the ability to activate your imagination. Please be assured that nothing will be done under hypnosis to cause you embarrassment or any discomfort. Quite the contrary, if you have the ability to focus your attention closely, and to accept suggestions without question or analysis, you will find hypnotic sleep and relaxation to be one of the most refreshing and delightful experiences in your entire life. As you drift into hypnotic relaxation, all signs of strain and tension disappear easily and gently. There is nothing supernatural or mystical about hypnosis. Instead, it is the most normal, natural, relaxing experience you can ever have. Your ability to be hypnotized has, in general, nothing to do with your intelligence or your strength of will. Also, it is impossible for you to be hypnotizzed without your full cooperation. There is no domination of will with hypnosis, instead the 'Power' of hypnosis is your power, or a special state of awareness, developed by you, and you alone. Hypnosis is something you do; it cannot be forced upon you. I can act only as a guide to suggest and outline the course you follow to attain relaxation of mind and body. Because you are always conscious, you will not allow yourself to do or say anything that is contrary to your will or moral code. If you should be left alone without instructions, or if you feel apprehensive, you can awaken yourself at any time, so have no fear or anxiety.

You must be sincere in the acceptance of hypnosis as a method of pain relief. Also you must have the desire and ability to cooperate and follow instructions without questioning or analyzing any of the statements or suggestions given you. Hypnosis can afford you relief from pain varying from partial to complete relief. This degree of relief will depend on you alone, and your ability to relax and to follow instructions in a willing and passive manner. When you awaken from hypnotic relaxation you will be more refreshed and more invigorated than you may have ever felt before. You will always find hypnosis refreshing and rejuvenating, leaving you relaxed and full of pep and energy with perfect cordination. Relaxation through hypnosis, is a short cut to better health and to greater happiness.

This leaflet presents information which actually conditions the patient for future trance inductions. In other words, it consists of a series of 'pre-hypnotic' suggestions.

Each patient is given a book to read such as: 'Childbirth Without Fear' by Grantly Dick Read, or 'Understanding Natural Childbirth' by Herbert Thoms. Also, from the 'Birth Atlas,' printed by the Maternity Center Association of New York, she is shown by actual pictures the process of fertilization, growth of the embryo and fetus, and finally the normal birth of a baby. In addition she is given physical exercises which include relaxation and breathing techniques for the different stages of labor; stretching of the pelvic floor; posture training, and exercises for figure-recovery after delivery. She is told of the changes which occur in the woman's body during pregnancy; some favorable and unfavorable symptoms; the relationship between emotional and physical health; breast feeding and nipple care, etc. If the patient desires, she is taken on a tour of the hospital and shown the labor, delivery, and postpartum rooms, and the nursery.

In my experience I have found that it is not necessary to start hypnotic training for childbirth until sometime after the sixth month of pregnancy. The first training session is a special thirty to forty-five minute appointment. At this time she listens to the following tape recording, which of course should be recorded using the physician's own voice. If more convenient, this may be read direct from the book. The patient should be made comfortable by placing a foam rubber mattress over the examination table. Outside office noises may be largely eliminated by the use of ear phones plugged into the tape recorder.

INTRODUCTION
(Tape Recording)

"Please make yourself comfortable, relax and close your eyes so that you can more easily concentrate on what I am going to tell you about relaxation and the nature of hypnosis. Now start to relax by taking a deep breath, in, in, in . . . relax as you exhale. Another deep breath, deeper, deeper, relax and exhale, and now continue to relax, each time as you exhale. You may change your position at any time you wish.

"Almost everyone would like to know how to relax easily. How pleasant life would be, if when anxiety and nervous tension develops, you could turn off an imaginary switch, and allow your mind and body to relax completely. Every natural process in the body is painless when it is functioning properly. Nervous tension frequently interferes with the functions of the body. Tension in itself, can be the cause of pain; for instance, the common headache is usually caused by 'nervous tension.' Nervous tension is the basic cause of stomach ulcers and many other conditions where there is muscular spasm and tension. Anxiety, fear and nervous tension can produce heart attacks and chest pain. Also skin diseases and allergic conditions are aggravated by tension. It may come as a surprise to most people that the discomfort of normal childbirth is almost negligible for the mother, if she is relaxed, and has no fear, anxiety, or tension. The dental chair also, holds little terror for the patient who is completly relaxed. Discomfort of any type is decreased when you are relaxed, both in mind and body. Relaxation is healing, relaxation is soothing and restful.

"Every woman wants her pregnancy and childbirth to be normal. The vast majority of births follow the normal and natural process. There is every reason for her to be assured that it will be normal when she is under the care of a competent doctor, in whom she has complete confidence. In childbirth the circular muscles of the lower part of the uterus relax, and allow the longitudinal muscles of the upper part of the uterus to contract and push the baby down through the birth canal. Tension may cause the circular

224

muscles of the lower part of the uterus (the cervix) to tighten up, so that not only are labor contractions painful, but also labor may be retarded. We know that labor is hard work, however, work does not need to be painful. Normal work can leave you pleasantly tired and relaxed.

"Briefly then, the pain of labor is due to tension caused by fear. The pain intensifies the fear, which in turn increases the tension by resistance of the muscles. And so the vicious circle of these three evils (tension, fear, and pain) destroys all confidence, relaxation, and self-control.

"Relaxation is the goal for which we are striving. With relaxation comes a feeling of self-control, confidence, security, contentment and well being. The sensation of complete relaxation while you are conscious, is the identical sensation you would have if you were under hypnotic relaxation and sleep. Hypnosis helps you to relax more completely than you can by any other method. The ability to completely relax is a skill which you can easily develop with practice. Our main purpose is to decrease tension, decrease anxiety, and the cares of every day living, so that you may enter into a bright *new* life of magnificent personal achievement.

"Every portion of this lesson will tend to make you feel more comfortable, and relaxed, light in spirit and in body. Every word, every thought will be directed to such a pleasant conclusion that you *will be* relaxed and rested, light in heart, buoyant, cheerful and happy.

"Now please *open* your eyes and continue to relax while I continue to talk. You may change your position at any time you wish, to make yourself comfortable. There are many ways to learn how to relax. For instance, if there is a light or any fixed point in front of you, please stare at it now, steadily; keep looking at it; look at it until your eyes become tired of it. If your gaze wanders away, look back at the object. This is only to help you concentrate more easily on thoughts of relaxation to be directed to you. Just listen and

225

record and accept the things I say, please do not try to analyze them. As I give you thoughts to think about, concentrate like this: If I should say that your arms feel very heavy, and that your arm and hand muscles are completely relaxed, just picture to yourself that your arms and hands *have become* heavy, heavy as lead, and are lying passively, without movement or strength, limp, relaxed, dull, and heavy. As you continue to relax, just let things happen as they happen, without any thought as to question or analysis. Please merely relax and follow instructions drifting deeper and deeper into pleasant relaxation.

"Now take a deep breath, in, in, in...and hold it while I count to five. 1-2-3-4-5, exhale, tell yourself relax deeply, let go. Now breathe normally...After the next deep breath, repeat to yourself, relax, relax, relax, as you exhale. Now take a deep breathe in, in, in...and hold it while I count to five again. 1-2-3-4-5...relax, relax, relax.

"Now please *close* your eyes gently but firmly. Squeeze the lids tightly together and hold them squeezed tightly together while you start *now* to take another deep breath...in, in, in, hold your breath and clench your eyes while I count to five. 1-2-3-4-5. Relax eyes, but keep them closed; exhale, relax, relax, relax. Now please keep your eyes closed; keep them closed and at the same time look up to an imaginary spot just above the forehead known as the relaxation center. With *closed* eye-lids keep looking up. When I have counted to five you will feel *very* relaxed. All right...1.—The scalp muscles are now relaxing; 2—your eyes and eyelids are relaxing; keep looking up; 3—your checks are relaxing; just let them droop and sag comfortably; 4—your chin is relaxing now; open the mouth slightly and wet your lips, then swallow; 5—now you are nicely relaxed; with eyelids closed keep looking up. I will count again to five and you will start to relax all over your body, and you will not want to open your eyes. 1—your eyes are closed but you are looking up at the relaxation center above your forehead; 2—your eyes feel very light, the eyelids feel very relaxed; they don't want to open; 3—you don't want to open your eyes, the lids feel as if they are glued together; keep looking up to relax them; 4—you don't want to open your eyes, eye-lids glued shut, sealed firmly together, heavy as lead, you can't open your eyes; 5—you are relaxed all over, just let all muscle tension flow out of your body; you don't want to open your eyes; eyelids sealed firmly; you can't open your eyes...the harder you try to open them, the heavier they feel. Now do not try to open them any more; just keep them closed and relaxed. They want to stay closed and relaxed. Please leave your eyes closed until I ask you to open them. Now thoroughly enjoy the soft pleasant relaxation of the quiet darkness. You are resting calmly and peacefully. Nothing will disturb your peaceful rest.

"Now let us relax every muscle in the body...First, relax the toes on your *right* foot. Let them go limp, limp, heavy, dull, and relaxed. Let this relaxation spread up through the arch of the foot...all the way to the ankle...so that your right foot is completely relaxed, relaxed and heavy, dull and limp. Now relax the toes on the *left* foot, the toes, the arch and the heel. Your left foot completely relaxed, relaxed and limp, limp and heavy, heavy and dull. Let this numbness and heaviness flow up the calf of your right leg. .so that you are now completely relaxed from the tip of your right toes to the knee. Now, let the left calf relax in the same manner...so that both feet and legs are completely relaxed up to the knees. Let the relaxation extend up through the large muscles of the right thigh...so that your right leg is completely relaxed up to the hip. Now let the left thigh also relax...so that your feet and legs are heavy, heavy and relaxed, relaxed and limp, limp and dull, dull, limp, and relaxed. So-o-o relaxed, so limp, so heavy, so numb. Now relax the fingers of the *right* hand. Feel them getting limp

227

and heavy, numb and relaxed. Notice the right hand relaxing more and more; getting more and more limp, more and more heavy. Now the fingers of the *left* hand are letting go completely, all the muscles relaxing, the fingers getting heavy, limp, dull, and relaxed. The left hand becoming relaxed and heavy. Now let that numb, heavy, relaxed feeling flow up the arms, the right forearm relaxed...the left forearm relaxed...the left upper arm relaxed...the right upper arm relaxed...both hands, both arms relaxed and heavy, heavy and limp, limp, and dull, and relaxed, all the way up to the shoulders. Now let the shoulders sag, limp, loose and relaxed. By this time you probably will notice a slight, pleasant *tingling* in the toes and fingers. This feeling will increase until you are completely bathed in a pleasant warm numb glow of utter relaxation. Now we are going to relax the body. The hips, the large back muscles, the abdomen, the chest muscles and the shoulders will all relax at once. We are going to take three deep breaths. Each time we exhale we will notice the body relaxing more and more. With the third deep breath will come a complete and dynamic relaxation over the entire body. Now breathe slowly in, in, in —Out, and relax completely. Now a deeper breath in, in, in—Out and *let go* completely. Now the third deep breath, in, in, in... Out and *completely relaxed*. Now you are breathing slowly, gently, deeply as a sleeper breathes. Every muscle in your chest, shoulders, back, abdomen and hips is completely relaxed and your whole body is heavy, heavy and numb, numb and warm, warm and limp, and heavy. Your arms and legs will continue to deepen this vague numbness and dullness. Your entire body will get more and more numb and dull and devoid of sensation. You may even become more and more unaware of your body as you go deeper and deeper into drowsy relaxation.

"You are now completely relaxed, your arms are relaxed, your legs are relaxed, your body is relaxed. Every muscle and nerve has responded, letting go completely. Your eyes are so sleeply, so drowsy. The lids are so heavy. All the muscles in your neck are now beginning to relax. Your head feels so heavy as the muscles release their tension. Let your jaw muscles relax so that your teeth do not quite touch ...Jaw muscles completely relaxed. Let all the muscles of the face and scalp relax completely. Let your shoulders sag, limp and relaxed. So limp, so heavy, so completely relaxed. As you become more and more relaxed you may notice certain changes within your body. You may even develop an unawareness, and forget the feeling in some part of your body.

"Now imagine yourself standing on a flight of steps. They may go up or they may go down, whichever you wish. That is unimportant. Count with me, to yourself, backwards from ten down to zero. With every count you will become drowsier and drowsier, as you relax more and more, deeper and deeper. Let yourself drift, floating and drifting down into pleasant, relaxing rest. When we reach zero, you will feel very drowsy, comfortable, pleasant and deeply relaxed. All right...10—you are becoming so relaxed, so relaxed all over. 9—getting so relaxed and drowsy-like, possibly sleepy. Let every muscle relax completely; just relax completely. 8— 7—relaxing. 6—becoming so calm and relaxed; so drowsy and relaxed. Let yourself just drift down into complete relaxation and comfort. 5— 4— 3—let yourself just drift down towards complete relaxation of mind and body. Rest. Relax. Every muscle so relaxed, so relaxed, and at complete ease. 2— 1—and zero. Now rest easily and gently. Easily and gently, trustingly, easily and gently. So relaxed, so drowsy and relaxed, pleasantly relaxed. Enjoy this feeling of well-being and ease.

"Please pay close attention to every suggestion that I give you. As you rest there all calm and quiet, your mind is awake and listening and receptive; it can concentrate easily and strongly upon every suggestion that I give you. All suggestions will be for your own good. You are resting calmly and quietly. Nothing will disturb you. No other sounds or voices will disturb your peaceful rest. You need pay no attention to other sounds for they are unimportant. Nothing will disturb you now. You can hear my voice clearly. No other sounds or voices will disturb your peaceful rest. You will find that you can easily and quickly and willingly follow every suggestion that I give you.

"With every breath that you take, every gentle, easy, regular breath, you are getting more deeply relaxed, deeper relaxed, deeper relaxed. Your eyes are closed. Please keep them closed until I tell you to open them. Your eyelids are stuck firmly together as if they were glued together. You are concentrating closely on every word that I speak, every suggestion that I give you. You are resting calmly and peacefully. Feeling very relaxed, so at ease. After this when you wish to really relax in our office, or at home, I suggest that you first make yourself comfortable. Then take a deep breath and let it out slowly and close your eyes and tell yourself to relax deeply. Immediately, you will notice that you *will* become *extremely* relaxed all over your body. After this when you wish to really relax, first make yourself comfortable, then take a deep breath and as you let it out slowly, close your eyes and tell yourself to relax deeply. Immediately, you will notice that you will become extremely relaxed all over your body, even more than you are now. And with every breath that you take you will relax more and more; deeper and deeper into relaxation. Automatically, as you exhale you will continue to relax more and more, deeper and deeper. Each time that you relax *like this*, you will be able to relax more easily, more quickly and more deeply. Relaxation is a skill which you can easily develop with practice.

"You have now attained our goal of relaxation, and with

230

it the feeling of self-control, confidence, security, contentment. At this very moment you are experiencing the same feelings and sensations you will be aware of when you are under hypnosis. It is a day-dreamy-like feeling where you are calm and relaxed. Although you are relaxed, drowsy and comfortable, you are also *definitely conscious*. You see, hypnosis is not like night sleep, because with hypnotic sleep and relaxation, you are *always* conscious and aware of things about you. Hypnosis is useful medically because you are conscious and you are able to cooperate and carry out suggestions that will be beneficial to you. Under hypnosis you are merely in a relaxed condition of increased suggestibility. Therefore, hypnosis acts to strengthen the effect of any suggestion. You must be able to concentrate, and most important you must have the ability to activate your imagination. Please be assured that nothing will be done under hypnosis to cause you embarrassment or any discomfortment. Quite the contrary, if you have the ability to focus your attention closely, and to accept suggestions without question or analysis, you will find hypnotic sleep and hypnotic relaxation to be one of the most refreshing and delightful experiences in your entire life. As you drift into hypnotic relaxation, all signs of strain and tension disappear easily and gently. Hereafter, whenever you wish to be hypnotized, you need *only* to relax and follow my instructions. Hereafter, whenever you wish to be hypnotized, you need only to relax and follow my instructions. There is nothing supernatural or mystical about hypnosis. Instead, it is the most normal, natural, relaxing experience you can ever have. Your ability to be hypnotized has, in general, nothing to do with your intelligence or your strength of will. Also, it is impossible for you to be hypnotized without your full cooperation. There is no domination of will with hypnosis. Instead, the 'Power' of hypnosis is your power, or a special state of awareness developed by you, and you

231

alone. Hypnosis is something you do; it cannot be forced upon you. I can only act as a guide to suggest and outline the course you follow to attain relaxation of mind and body. Because you are always conscious, you will not allow yourself to do or say anything that is contrary to your will or moral code. If you should be left alone, without instructions, or if you feel apprehensive, you can awaken yourself at any time, so have no fear or anxiety.

"You must be sincere in the acceptance of hypnosis as a method of pain relief. Also, you must have the desire and ability to cooperate and to follow instructions without questioning or analyzing any of the statements given you. Hypnosis can afford you relief from pain varying from partial to complete relief. This degree of relief will depend on you alone, and your ability to relax, and follow instructions in a willing and passive manner. Hereafter, whenever you wish to be hypnotized, you need *only* to relax and follow my instructions. Merely relax and follow instructions.

"In a few moments I am going to ask you to awaken from this relaxation sleep. When you awaken you will be more refreshed and more invigorated than you have ever felt before. You will always find hypnosis relaxing, refreshing, and invigorating, leaving you relaxed and full of pep and energy with perfect coordination. I am going to count to three. *AFTER* the count of three your eyes will open. On the count of three you are alert, vital, vigorous and perfectly refreshed; refreshed as though you are awakening from a long nap. All right, now, here we go...1—you are starting to awaken now, and beginning to feel life, energy and vigor flowing into your arms, your legs and body. Your eyes feel fresh and clear. From head to foot you are feeling perfect, physically perfect, mentally perfect, emotionally perfect. 2—you are more and more awake, you feel vigorous, energetic, perfect from head to foot. You are complete-

ly refreshed, rejuvenated. Your eyes are all ready to open. 3—Eyes open, WIDE AWAKE!"
(Instruct patient ahead of time how to turn off the tape recorder.)

During the second training period (half-an-hour) she is taught a simple method of relaxation, and also hypnosis is induced. This method of relaxation is a modification of the 'Decubitus Exercise' as described by Frederick Pierce in his book entitled, 'Mobilizing the Mid-Brain.' Pierce attributes the effectiveness of this exercise to the following facts. 1. Muscles relax more completely when the conscious attention is withdrawn. 2. A muscle relaxed by withdrawing attention, tends to remain below its normal conscious tone, until attention is again specifically directed to it. 3. Muscles relax more completely when they have previously been placed under a load. Briefly, then, the technique may be summarized in the following manner. First, muscles are placed under stress. At a given signal they are released from this stress and simultaneously the attention is detached from the muscles. The effectiveness of this technique in promoting relaxation is shown by the fact that approximately 75 per cent of all patients will spontaneously drift into hypnosis without any other suggestions being given. If suggestions for hypnotic induction are given at the end of the exercise, (as illustrated below) hypnosis can be induced easily in almost 100 per cent of the patients.

PRE-INDUCTION EXERCISE

"There are many ways to learn how to relax. Many of us unconsciously release nervous tension by simply taking a deep breath and then as we exhale, allow the body to slump into relaxation and become limp. Today I am going to teach you a simple, rapid and extremely effective routine to follow for complete relaxation of body and mind. It is something you can use in your everyday life." (At this point remove high-heel shoes)

"Please make yourself comfortable. Sit back in the chair and place both feet flat on the floor. Now please close your eyes so that you can more easily concentrate on what I am saying. You may open your eyes anytime you wish, if you should feel uneasy. However, I would prefer that you keep them closed so that you can fully cooperate without any distractions.

"Now slowly take a deep breath, in, in, in, and hold it for a moment. As you exhale now, say to yourself, relax, let go, relax. Now take in a second deep breath, in, in, in, hold it for a moment. Exhale and relax completely, let go. Now a third deep full breath, in, in, in, exhale and completely relax, limp and relaxed.

"Now let your head sag all the way forward, relaxed. Then let it fall over slowly to the right shoulder. Notice the pulling and stretching of the muscles. Head now continuing slowly on around all the way back, feeling the muscles pull and stretch. Now head moving slowly over to the left shoulder, muscles pull and stretch. And now head around front completely relaxed. Please repeat a second time slowly. Just feel the muscles pull and stretch as they become more loose. Pulling and stretching as the head rotates slowly. It feels so good to let the muscles relax. Muscles stretching and pulling. And now around front, muscles relaxed. Now a third time, that's right, notice how much more relaxed the muscles are this time. Pulling and stretching, then relaxing. Slowly around, pulling and stretching. And now around front completely relaxed. Now around the opposite direction to the left shoulder, slowly. Just feel the muscles pulling and stretching, pulling and stretching. More and more relaxed. Pulling and stretching, then around front completely relaxed. The second time now, slowly around. Muscles pulling and stretching, loosening and relaxing. It feels so good to let muscles relax. Pulling and stretching, slowly. Pulling and stretching, and now around front relaxed completely. Now the last time around slowly, letting all tension and tightness flow out completely. Muscles pulling and stretching. So relaxed, pulling and stretching. And now around front, completely relaxed. The head may assume any position that is comfortable. Chin up slightly to keep the neck muscles relaxed. Continue to breathe easily and gently, as a sleeper breathes, easily and gently. Becoming more and more relaxed each time as you exhale, easily and gently.

"Now please straighten out your right (or left) leg, so that the knee is stiff and the heel is high off the floor. Toes pulled back. Almost immediately notice the tightness, cramping and fatigue of the calf muscles. This discomfort will increase more and more. Also the knee and thigh muscles are becoming tight, tense and tired. The leg more and more unsteady. Imagine the load getting heavier and heavier. When I give the signal which is the word 'RELAX,' let the entire right (or left) side of you body go limp and loose, and at the same time let your foot *fall* to the floor absolutely limp. All right... 'RELAX!' Now please straighten out your left leg. (continue as above substituting *Left*).

"Please extend the right (or left) arm out straight in front of you. Elbow stiff; fingers extended; palm down. Imagine a heavy weight placed on the back of the hand, so that the arm is now under a load getting heavier and heavier. Muscles of the lower arm responding, getting more and more tense, more and more tired. Upper arm tense, tired and heavy, more and more tired, heavier and heavier. Now notice the shoulders and how the pulling, drawing and strained feeling is increasing as the load is getting heavier and heavier. This discomfort will increase as the arm becomes more tired and more fatigued. The arm now getting more and more unsteady, as it becomes heavier and heavier. When I give the signal to relax this time, let

235

the entire right (left) side of the body relax and go limp and loose, and at the same time let your arm fall into your lap, absolutely limp. All right 'RELAX!' Now please extend the left arm." (continue as above substituting *Left*). Continue to breathe easily and gently, easily and gently, becoming more and more relaxed each time as you exhale. Resting easily and calmly, calmly and peacefully.

"Now I would like for you to imagine a large blackboard in front of you. I am going to draw a circle on this blackboard. The circle is about three feet in diameter. With your eyes closed, start at the top of the circle and go around it with your eyes slowly, three times to the right, then slowly three times to the left. Just nod when you finish. Now imagine another blackboard in front of you. On this one I am going to draw a square. It is about three feet on each side. With closed eyes start at the right upper corner and go around it with your eyes slowly, three times to the right, then slowly three times to the left. Nod when you finish. Now on another blackboard I am going to draw a figure of eight. Start at the top and go around it slowly three times to the right, then slowly three times to the left. Nod when you finish.

"If you feel like taking a deep breath now, please do so and relax completely. Continue to relax now as you breathe easily and gently. Relaxing more and more each time as you exhale. Going deeper and deeper into peaceful relaxation, deeper and deeper, more and more relaxed. Each time you exhale becoming more and more relaxed. Rest. Relax. Feeling safe and secure, resting easily and gently, deeper and deeper. Being aware only of my voice and your breathing. Concentrate and focus all your attention on your breathing, exhale and relax, exhale and relax, exhale and relax. As you go deeper and deeper and become more and more relaxed you may notice certain changes within your body. You may even forget the feeling in some part of your body. Arms and legs heavy and relaxed, dull and limp. So heavy, so relaxed. Resting easily and gently, going deeper and deeper each time as you exhale, deeper and deeper.

"At this very moment you are experiencing the same feelings and sensations that you are aware of when you are under hypnosis. You see, hypnosis is not like night sleep, because with hypnotic sleep you are always conscious and aware of things about you. Because you are relaxed you are now able to cooperate and carry out suggestions easily. In a few moments I am going to ask you to open your eyes. I'll tell you exactly when. After you give me your permission, I will guide you into hypnosis quickly and easily. You will then feel and be aware of things exactly the same as you are now, except that you will be more relaxed and even more comfortable and receptive to suggestions. You will be able to drift into hypnotic relaxation easily and gently. I can easily see that you are a good hypnotic subject because you have responded more quickly than usual to this relaxation. Because you responded so easily, I am going to use a rapid but pleasant method to induce hypnosis."

(Select any method for induction you wish, e.g. spiral, coin, ring. However give patient a general idea of the method and the effects it will produce on her. This is valuable as it conditions the patient by giving her 'pre-hypnotic' suggestions. I prefer to use a rotating spiral, or the rapid finger motion).

"The method I'll use, is to have your eyes follow the movements of my fingers going up and down, up and down, up and down. Within a very few moments you will notice that your eyelids will become heavier and heavier. It will become more and more difficult to follow my fingers as the lids get heavier and heavier, heavier and heavier. Your eyes may go slightly out of focus, and you may even feel the desire to swallow. When your eyelids get too heavy to hold open any longer, just let the heavy lids close and relax. As your lids close, you will drift quickly into complete relaxation, the same as you are now; continuing to go deeper and deeper as I talk to you. Now as I count to three, please let your eyes open. You will of course feel drowsy and relaxed, but you can cooperate easily. All right, 1—2—3. Eyes open. You certainly have responded well! Would you like to have me hypnotize you now? That's fine."

(Hold hand six inches from patient's face, extend index and middle fingers. Keep remaining fingers in palm of hand. Wave fingers up and down through a fifteen inch arc, primarily with a wrist motion. Keep the stroke rate just as rapid as patient can follow with her eyes so that she occasionally misses a stroke. When she misses a stroke, slow down enough, so that she can pick up the rate again).

"Now please hold your head still and watch the end of my fingers closely. As your eyes follow my finger tips, the lids will rapidly get heavier and heavier, tired and heavy, tired and heavy. Harder to hold open, more and more heavy, heavier and heavier. Eyes slightly out of focus, heavier and heavier, heavier and heavier. Lids closing now, heavier and heavier, closing and heavy, closing and heavy, closing, closing, closing, too heavy to hold open." (Repeat suggestions until lids shut voluntarily. If patient fights to keep lids open, or if fluttering occurs, merely ask the patient to close lids to the count of 1—2—3.

Every patient is taught self-hypnosis, and instructed to use it at least two or three times daily. Also during this session she is given a signal to facilitate future inductions, so that she will fall into hypnosis on command. She is informed that this signal will work anywhere, even over the telephone. However, she *must always* give her permission first. I use this signal on all patients, *"Sleep now, 1—2—3."*

A minimum of fifteen to thirty minutes should be allowed for all subsequent hypnotic training periods. Usually four

238

to six sessions, after the second session, are adequate to train the average good subject. More frequent visits and additional time will be necessary when special problems arise. Abreaction (ventilation of an emotional experience) is employed to relieve the patient of fears related to her inability to develop complete anesthesia or analgesia by the usual methods. If complete numbness cannot be developed, always ask her, under hypnosis, why she thinks this did not occur. Also ask what suggestions would help her to obtain absolute numbness. Invariably she will give you the correct answer. During these subsequent visits emphasis is placed on deepening the trance. Under hypnosis she is told just what feelings, and sensations and experiences she may expect during labor and delivery. Therefore, if and when they do occur, they will not seem to be new experiences to her. During at least two antepartum sessions the patient is asked to carry out suggestions under hypnosis with her eyes open, e.g., getting a drink of water, going to the bathroom, or any little errand. Under hypnosis, all patients are examined vaginally a week or so prior to term. The husband is encouraged to attend at least one of the training sessions. His permission should always be obtained before hypnotic training is started.

A patient can endure the rigors of labor and delivery (including episiotomy, posterior colporrhaphy, perineorrhaphy, digital exploration of uterine cavity and cervical repair) without pain or discomfort, by one of two methods. First, by being able to develop complete analgesia or anaesthesia from her knees to her chest as outlined by Cooke. Second, by developing a lack of awareness of her body, or a detached feeling from her body. It is suggested that it will seem to her that she is somewhere in the labor or delivery room, merely looking on as an interested observer. It will be similar to watching a motion picture of childbirth. For this second method to be completely effective the patient must develop a moderate degree of numbness. Naturally childbirth under hypnosis is much easier for the patient if her physician is in constant attendance. However, this is not absolutely necessary. Transference of guidance may easily be given to a nurse, intern, resident, with re-inforcement from her own physician only from time to time. The re-inforcement can easily be given by telephone if necessary.

The following post-hypnotic suggestions are repeated several times to all patients under hypnosis, during the training sessions.

1. The only things you will remember about labor and delivery are the pleasant things. You will remember all the pleasant things clearly.

2. Time will pass quickly and pleasantly, and there will be no fatigue or exhaustion, because of your deep relaxation.

3. As labor advances you will develop more courage and confidence.

4. Labor contractions will only reach a certain peak, thereafter you will always be able to handle them easily and with courage.

5. Labor is hard work and if it helps to utter slight grunting noises, that will be all right, as it releases tension.

6. You will be able to move about in bed, and use the bedpan or toilet and still stay deeply hypnotized. Opening your eyes will not awaken you.

7. Other noises or voices will not disturb you, instead they will act as signals to deepen your hypnosis.

8. There will be no nausea, sickness or pain during or after labor.

9. As the baby's head passes down through the birth canal there may be sensations of pushing, stretching, expansion, pulling, drawing, urge to have a bowel movement, suprapubic pressure, trembling of legs, back pressure, but there will be no pain associated with any of these.

240

10. All during labor, repeat to yourself, relax, calm, numb, courage.

11. You will be able to go deeper into hypnosis during labor than ever before. Every breath and every uterine contraction will be a signal for you to go deeper and deeper into hypnosis.

12. You will always be informed ahead of time when any procedure is done for you. Everything will be explained to you.

13. You will be able to decrease the flow of blood from the episiotomy, by making the vessels contract.

14. Watching the birth of the baby will be very interesting and thrilling. Seeing the blood and secretions will have no effect on you, other than being interesting.

15. You will be able to keep the numbness in the area of your stitches until they are all healed. Stitches numb!

16. After labor is over, you will feel only pleasantly tired, so that you can relax and sleep easily at any time while in the hospital.

17. During and after the delivery you will always be happy, courageous, and calm, with a wonderful feeling of accomplishment.

18. Because you will be relaxed and happy there will be no 'maternity blues,' instead only a calm, happy, contented, relaxed feeling.

19. After delivery if rectal pain develops, or if after-contractions are annoying, you will be able to numb that area.

20. On returning to your room after delivery, you will drift immediately into a deep normal night sleep. When you awaken you will be completely refreshed, wide awake, and feel physically, mentally, and emotionally perfect, with only pleasant memories of your labor and delivery.

21. When labor begins, the contractions will hurt. How-

ever, after you arrive at the hospital the contrations will not be painful.

22. Suggestions for natural childbirth as outlined by Cooke should also be given.

(Include any other suggestions that your particular patient requires).

Post-partum instructions, when given under hypnosis, are carried out faithfully and are much more effective than when given in the waking state. Drying-up lactation can be usually accomplished by merely having the patient carry out the following routine four times a day under auto-hypnosis. Have patient place her hands over her breasts and make gentle but firm pressure as she counts slowly, to herself, from one to ten. While counting, she is to give herself suggestions to the effect that the blood supply is decreasing and getting less and less to the breasts; breast getting more and more numb; glandular tissue shrinking down, getting smaller and smaller so that it is unable to form milk; by the count of ten the glands will shrink down to just a small dot (suggest that the glandular tissue looks similar to a cluster of grapes). If you desire for her to *increase* her milk supply, have her go through a similar routine, except have her suggest the following: warmth from her hands is increasing the blood supply to the breasts, blood vessals dilating, getting larger and larger; glandular tissue (grape-like clusters) getting larger and larger, so that more milk can be formed; each time she nurses the milk will flow in easily and in large amounts, etc.

Hypnosis is employed prior to the sixth month of pregnancy when the patient complains of nausea, vomiting, excessive salivation, insomnia, emotional instability, excessive fatigue, etc.

In *summary* then, the patient is conditioned for hypnosis with reading material and a tape recording. On her second visit she is taught how to relax and hypnosis is induced.

242

Subsequent visits are devoted to deepening the trance, developing numbness, and giving her post-hypnotic suggestions for childbirth.

If hypnosis can be as effective as narcotics and barbiturates in alleviating anxiety and pain during childbirth, then it would certainly appear to be a very valuable asset in the care of an obstetrical patient. In patients who respond well to hypnosis, I find that because they can actively cooperate, hypnosis is much superior to drug sedation. It can also supplant the use of an anaesthetic in good hypnotic subjects, in about twenty-five to fifty percent of the patients.

Instead of a mother experiencing a 'blackout' during childbirth, hypnosis allows her to actively participate in a thrilling experience, without the aid of drugs or an anaesthetic. Even more important, there is no drug depression of respiration in the newborn.

I have utilized a modification of the Grantly Dick Read technique of 'natural childbirth' with success in about 165 patients. (Currently this method is used only to a limited degree.) Several of these patients have subsequently been delivered under hypnosis. Almost without exception these patients enthusiastically prefer hypnosis. As they state: there is less fatigue and nervous exhaustion, relaxation is easier and much deeper, an anaesthetic is not required for the episiotomy and the repair, the stitches are not painful, and they have more energy and vitality during the entire recovery period.

The intelligent use of hypnosis allows her greater mastery of her emotions and feelings in her everyday living. Anxiety, tension and apprehension can therefore be tremendously decreased. It becomes obvious then, that hypnosis affords many major benefits and advantages to the obstetrical patient. Physicians should make every effort to eliminate the cause of fear, anxiety and pain of childbirth.

REFERENCES

1. Ahlheim, V., *The Truth About Hypnotism*, New Age Publishing Co., 1947.

2. Bennett, C., *Hypnotic Power*, New York: Dutton, 1937.

3. Bernheim, H., *Suggestive Therapeutics*, London Book Co., 1889, reprinted, 1947.

4. Bramwell, M., *Hypnotism*, New York: J. R. Lippencott Co., 1928.

5. Brenman, M., and Gill, M. M. *Hypnotherapy*, International Universities Press, 1947.

6. Cannon, A., *The Science of Hypnotism*, New York: Dutton, 1936.

7. Cook, W. W., *Practical Lessons in Hypnotism*, Willey Book Co., 1943 (1901).

8. Dane, V., *How to Hypnotize Yourself and Others*, Marcel Rodd Co., 1946.

9. Davis, L. W., and Husband, R. W., "A Study of Hypnotic Susceptibility in Relation to Personality Traits," *Journal of Abnormal and Social Psychology*, 26: 175-182 (1931).

10. Erickson, M. H., *Hypnosis in Medicine*, Medical Clinics of North America, Vol. 28, No. 3, May 1944, page 639.

11. Estabrooks, G. H., *Hypnotism*, New York: E. P. Dutton & Co., 1943.

12. Hayakawa, S. I., *Language in Action*, New York: Harcourt, Brace & Co., 1941.

13. Horsley, J. S., *Narco-Analysis*, Oxford University Press, 1943.

14. Hudson, T. J., *The Law of Psychic Phenomena*, A. C. McClurg & Co., 1897.

15. Hull, C. L., *Hypnosis and Suggestibility*, New York: Appleton-Century Co., 1933.

16. Johnson, Wendell, *People in Quandaries*, New York: Harpers, 1946.

17. Kahn, S., *Suggestion and Hypnosis Made Practical*, Meador Publishing Co., 1945.

18. Korzybski, Alfred, *Science and Sanity*, Lancaster, Pa.: The Science Press Printing Co., 1941.

19. Kuhn, L. and Russo, S., *Modern Hypnosis*, Psychological Library, 1947.

20. LeCron, Leslie M., Ed., *Experimental Hypnosis*, New York: The Macmillan Co., 1954.

21. LeCron, Leslie M., and Bordeaux, J.,*Hypnotism Today*, New York: Grune & Stratton, 1947.

22. Lee, Irving J. *Language Habits in Human Affairs*, New York: Harpers, 1941.

23. Lindner, R., *Rebel Without a Cause*, New York: Grune & Stratton, 1944.

24. Marks, R. W., *The Story of Hypnotism*, New York: Prentice-Hall, 1947.

25. Menninger, Karl, *The Human Mind*, New York: Knopf, 1945.

26. Moll, A., *Hypnotism*, London: Walter Scott, 1891.

27. Moore, Wilbur E., "Hypnosis in a System of Therapy for Stutterers," *Journal of Speech Disorders*, Vol. XI, 1946, p. 117-122.

28. Pavlov, Ivan P., *Lectures on Conditioned Reflexes, Vol. II: Conditioned Reflexes and Psychiatry*, New York: International Publishers, 1941.

29. Read, G. D., *Childbirth Without Fear*, New York: Harpers, 1944.

30. Salter, A., *What is Hypnosis?* Richard R. Smith, 1944.

31. Seabury, David, *How Jesus Heals Our Minds Today*, Boston: Little, 1940.

32. Shaw, S. I., *Hypnotism Can Help*, David McKay Co., 1948.

33. Snyder, Edward D., *Hypnotic Poetry*, University of Pennsylvania Press, 1930.

34. Watkins, John G., *Hypnotherapy of War Neuroses*, New York: Grune & Stratton, 1945.

35. Weiss, Edward, and Spurgeon, O., *Psychosomatic Medicine*, New York: W. B. Saunders Co., 1943.

36. Wolberg, L. R., *Hypnoanalysis*, New York: Grune & Stratton, 1945.

37. Wolberg, L. R., *Medical Hypnosis*, New York: Grune & Stratton, 1948, 2 Vols.

38. Wolfe, B., and Rosenthal, R., *Hypnotism Comes of Age*, New York: Bobbs-Merrill, 1948.

39. Young, L. E., *The Science of Hypnotism*, Baltimore: Ottenheimer, 1899.

HYPNOSIS BIBLIOGRAPHY

In the following bibliography, the authors have rated each book for its possible usefulness to the student of psychotherapy and hypnotherapy.

    ****   Highly recommended
    ***   Recommended
    **   Of little value
    *   Not recommended

** Ahlheim, V., *The Truth About Hypnotism*, New Age Publishing Co., 1947.
This 80 page volume presents one technique in detail. The theory presented is chiefly based on the works of the very early writers. The technique is dominating.

* Bennett, C.,*Hypnotic Power*, New York: Dutton, 1937, The view point of this book is dated far earlier than the date of publication. It is slightly metaphysical and reflects the opinions of the "early writers."

** Bernheim, H., *Suggestive Therapeutics*, London Book Co., 1889, reprinted 1947. Historically very interesting because in this work the theories of suggestion and the relationships between suggestion and the "animal magnetic" and "hypnotic" phenomena are crystalized and clearly established.

** Bramwell, M., *Hypnotism*, New York: J. R. Lippencott Co., 1928. One of the more recent classics of hypnotic literature from the view point of the clinician. Some of his case histories are very interesting.

*** Brenman, M., and Gill, M. M., *Hypnotherapy*, International Universities Press, 1947. A survey of the literature, some case histories and some original work, done by a psychologist and a physician who are skilled in the practice of hypnosis. Parts of it are written in highly academic form which makes reading slightly difficult.

* Cannon, A., *The Science of Hypnotism*, New York: Dutton, 1936. Cannon is renowned for his interest in and writings on metaphysics. It is very doubtful if many scientific therapists will to agree with him.

* Cook, W. W., *Practical Lessons in Hypnotism*, Willey Book Co., 1943 (1901). This is one of the more "horrible" examples of the way some publishers have attempted to exploit the revival of interest in hypnosis. The copyright date (1901) is printed in Roman numerals, the reprint date in Arabic. Careless buyers note the more recent date and assume that the book is modern. It is to be found in almost every bookstore, and is approximately as useful to the modern hypnotherapist as would be a physics text of 1850 to a researcher in nuclear fission.

*** Dane, V., *How to Hypnotize Yourself and Others*, Marcel Rodd Co., 1946. Mr. Dane complains that in cutting his original 70,000 word manuscript to 40,000 words, the publishers have "ruined" his book. Although some of the concepts in this book seem to be influenced by Dane's experiences in the Orient, most of his theory and all of his techniques are acceptable.

*** Estabrooks, G. H., *Hypnotism*, New York: E. P. Dutton & Co., 1943. This book, which has been both criticized and commended, was for some time the best modern book on hypnosis. Although over-shadowed by more recent works, it is still worth reading.

**** Horsley, J. S., *Narco-analysis,* Oxford University Press, 1943. This book is a *must* for the physician who uses hypnosis. It is highly recommended for dentists who use sodium pentothal. Sections of it are of interest to the psychotherapist.

** Hudson, T. J., *The Law of Psychic Phenomena,* A. C. McClurg & Co., 1897. Historically interesting. Some case histories and techniques might prove useful. The therory is worthless in light of later discoveries. The same comment might be made on all books on hypnosis published in this era or earlier.

** Hull, C. L., *Hypnosis and Suggestibility,* New York: Appleton-Century Co., 1933. A pioneer work in the scientific investigation of hypnosis as a psychological phenomena. The approach is statistical, the experiments are fairly well controlled. As reading, it is somewhat dull and of little interest to the therapist who wishes a practical, rather than theoretical understanding of hypnosis. More recent developments have made much of this work obsolete.

** Kahn, S., *Suggestion and Hypnosis Made Practical,* Meador Publishing Co., 1945. This book is written for the layman rather than for the therapist. It rambles over the general field of psychotherapy with emphasis on suggestion and hypnosis.

*** Kuhn, L., and Russo, S., *Modern Hypnosis,* Psychological Library, 1947. An excellent symposium presenting papers which have appeared in the various psychological and psychiatric journals. The editors have contributed nothing original, but have made an excellent choice of material.

**** LeCron, Leslie M., Ed., *Experimental Hypnosis,* New York: The Macmillan Co., 1954. This symposium consists of papers by many outstanding leaders in the modern development of therapeutic hypnosis. It contains invaluable information for the student of hypnosis.

**** LeCron, Leslie M., and Bordeaux, J., *Hypnotism Today,* New York: Grune and Stratton, 1947. An excellent text book on the theory and practice of therapeutic hypnosis. The foreword by Milton Erickson is highly significant. The book is modern in outlook and properly considers hypnosis as a method of implementing psychotherapy rather than as a therapy per se.

**** Lindner, R., *Rebel Without a Cause,* New York: Grune and Stratton, 1944. In this single case history Lindner gives a fine example of the way in which hypnosis can be used to speed up a classical Freudian psychoanalysis. So little of the book is devoted to hypnosis per se that it is of little general interest. For the psychoanalyst, psychotherapist or counselor.

* Marks, R. W., *The Story of Hypnotism,* New York: Prentice-Hall, 1947. A biased survey of the literature by a writer who shows his lack of personal experience with the science. Rather badly slanted in spots and incomplete in coverage.

** Moll, A., *Hypnotism,* London: Walter Scott, 1891. Interesting because it is the work of one of the great pioneers in psychiatry.

*** Salter, A., *What is Hypnosis?* Richard R. Smith, 1944. An attempt to equate hypnosis with Pavlov's "Conditioned Reflex." In this he is unsuccessful and so

250

does not answer the question in his title. He does illustrate the use of hypnosis in establishing conditioned reflexes and gives three methods of teaching autohypnosis.

* Shaw, S. I., *Hypnotism Can Help*, David McKay Co., 1948. Dr. Shaw, a dentist, has given us a modern example of the type of hypnotherapy which caused hypnosis to lose standing as a therapy at the turn of the century. He mentions only one technique for hypnotizing, works only on subjects who respond quickly and easily, and casually tells about "curing" the symptoms of deep-seated psychological disturbances in several short hypnotic "treatments." This is an example of well-intentioned "symptom treatment" by a sincere, but misguided, "hypnotist."

*** Snyder, Edward D., *Hypnotic Poetry*, University of Pennsylvania Press, 1930. Although of little clinical value, this study of the hypnotic effect of word sounds, tempo, meter and rhythm is of great interest to the technical researcher.

**** Watkins, John G., *Hypnotherapy of War Neuroses*, New York: Ronald Press, 1949. An excellent presentation of the modern approach to hypnotherapy, although his studies are based entirely on military psychotherapy. The principles illustrated lend themselves to many applications in civilian psychotherapy.

**** Wolberg, L. R., *Hypnoanalysis*, New York: Grune & Stratton, 1945. An outstanding work by an outstanding man. Half of the book is devoted to a single case history, an account of the "impossible," but successful reintegration of a psychotic patient, by means of hypnotherapy. The balance of the book is devoted to a discussion of theory and technique in the various phases of hypnotherapy.

**** Wolberg, L. R., *Medical Hypnosis*, New York: Grune & Stratton, 1948, 2 Vols. A comprehensive and authoritative work on therapeutic hypnosis. It contains a great deal of original work, well illustrated with case histories. The vocabulary is highly technical. A thorough understanding of psychoanalytic theory is expected of the reader. For the psychoanalyst, psychiatrist, or advanced student of psychotherapy.

*** Wolfe, B., and Rosenthal, R., *Hypnotism Comes of Age*, New York: Bobbs-Merrill, 1948. An excellent and unbiased survey of the literature of hypnosis. Although the authors are writers, not psychotherapists, and have no personal contribution to make to the science, they have done an excellent job of research and have presented the material in a book which is both easily read and scientifically sound.

* Young, L. E., *The Science of Hypnotism*. Baltimore: Ottenheimer, 1899. Another example of the current reprinting of a hopelessly obsolete book. It is a compilation of the works of the experimenters of the last century.